Domain Analysis for Knowledge Organization

T0383256

CHANDOS

INFORMATION PROFESSIONAL SERIES

Series Editor: Ruth Rikowski
(email: Rikowskigr@aol.com)

Chandos' new series of books is aimed at the busy information professional. They have been specially commissioned to provide the reader with an authoritative view of current thinking. They are designed to provide easy-to-read and (most importantly) practical coverage of topics that are of interest to librarians and other information professionals. If you would like a full listing of current and forthcoming titles, please visit www.chandospublishing.com.

New authors: we are always pleased to receive ideas for new titles; if you would like to write a book for Chandos, please contact Dr Glyn Jones on g.jones.2@elsevier.com or telephone +44 (0) 1865 843000.

Domain Analysis for Knowledge Organization

Tools for Ontology Extraction

Richard P. Smiraglia

AMSTERDAM • BOSTON • CAMBRIDGE • HEIDELBERG
LONDON • NEW YORK • OXFORD • PARIS • SAN DIEGO
SAN FRANCISCO • SINGAPORE • SYDNEY • TOKYO
Chandos Publishing is an imprint of Elsevier

CHANDOS
PUBLISHING

Chandos Publishing is an imprint of Elsevier
225 Wyman Street, Waltham, MA 02451, USA
Langford Lane, Kidlington, OX5 1GB, UK

Notices
Knowledge and best practice in this field are constantly changing. As new research and experience broaden our understanding, changes in research methods, professional practices, or medical treatment may become necessary.

Practitioners and researchers must always rely on their own experience and knowledge in evaluating and using any information, methods, compounds, or experiments described herein. In using such information or methods they should be mindful of their own safety and the safety of others, including parties for whom they have a professional responsibility.

To the fullest extent of the law, neither the Publisher nor the authors, contributors, or editors, assume any liability for any injury and/or damage to persons or property as a matter of products liability, negligence or otherwise, or from any use or operation of any methods, products, instructions, or ideas contained in the material herein.

ISBN: 978-0-08-100150-9

British Library Cataloguing in Publication Data
A catalogue record for this book is available from the British Library

Library of Congress Control Number: 2015935167

For information on all Chandos Publishing visit our
website at http://store.elsevier.com/

Working together
to grow libraries in
developing countries

www.elsevier.com • www.bookaid.org

Contents

List of figures and tables

List of figures

List of tables

Acknowledgments

As usual this book involves the interaction of many scholars. I would like to acknowledge Dr. Ingetraut Dahlberg, for the opportunity to engage the science she created at its most critical level by serving for a decade as editor of its formal journal *Knowledge Organization*, and now for the opportunity to write about her work.

More specific thanks must go to Laura Ridenour who helped with visualizations, particularly those in Chapters 2 and 6. I am indebted to Melodie Fox and Daniel Martinez-Avila for helping me gain access to sources in critical theory and discourse analysis, although I have done them short shrift in this volume.

All illustrations and quotations are properly documented; my access to the *Web of Science* was through the subscription of the University of Wisconsin, Milwaukee; my access to *Scopus* was through the subscription of Long Island University. It has been my privilege for the past three decades (LIU 1992–2009; UWM 2009) to serve as professor of knowledge organization at both of these institutions.

Discourse domains and their role in knowledge production dissemination and organization

1

1.1 Domain analysis for knowledge organization

This book is about domain analysis for knowledge organization. We take the term "knowledge organization," often represented as KO in these pages, to mean the science of the order of knowledge and its application in knowledge organization systems (KOSs). Elsewhere (Smiraglia, 2014) I have defined knowledge as that which is known, and suggested that the science of knowledge organization is concerned not only with the metalevel multi- and interdisciplinary comprehension of knowledge but also with the heuristics for the conceptual ordering of that which is known. Research in knowledge organization takes place in many arenas, from the philosophical to the basics of every science. Because ordering knowledge is an essential aspect of the development of systems for information retrieval, often we find a focus on knowledge that is recorded in documents. But this need not be a formal criterion for the science of knowledge organization. We may study the heuristics for the ordering of concepts in documents, but we also may study the heuristics by which natural phenomena (such as biological phenomena) seem to be ordered, or to order themselves in reality. Thus, in KO, we are concerned with the ability to study the natural order of phenomena in every context—a frighteningly complex context for research.

However, the science of knowledge organization has emerged from centuries of practice—taxonomy and typology for certain, but also epistemology and ontology, and the evolution of controlled vocabularies (thesauri) and symbolic notational systems (classifications). In every instance, we require empirical understanding about the knowledge bases of contexts. In the science of knowledge organization as it has evolved from proposals by Dahlberg (2006), the search for atomic knowledge elements has focused on concepts. Concepts are themselves complex, (Smiraglia and van den Heuvel, 2013; Hjørland, 2009), and their constitutional aspects must also be comprehended. Toward the end of the twentieth century, the KO community turned to a postmodern view of knowledge (Mai 1994; Smiraglia 2012) in which domain-centric points of view and interoperability among them replaced the search for global (universal, catholic, unitary, etc.) systems. In this new reality domain analysis, or the study of the knowledge bases of specific, definable contexts, has become a core paradigm within the knowledge organization community. This book is about specific techniques, primarily those that are empirical, for discovering, documenting, and analyzing domains.

1.2   Catalysts for domain-analytical thought

From about the mid-1990s knowledge organization has been focused on efforts to interpret diverse domains and points of view (epistemologies) together, or in tandem, rather than continuing to seek a single universally applicable approach to the organization of all human knowledge. Mai (1999) was among the first to call for such a post-modern view of knowledge organization and its use as an approach to KOSs. Explaining the modern view that the role of knowledge organization was to represent (if, in fact, it could discover) the actual order of things in the universe of which humanity was a part, Mai suggested a distinction between a modern approach to knowledge organization based on discovery of ontology and a postmodern, existentialist approach to knowledge organization based on epistemology, or the points of view of diverse groups of people. Postmodern approaches acknowledge that a KOS is itself just one single point of view about a particular knowledge set, that other points of view can coexist and could be formed into KOSs, and finally that the role of postmodern knowledge organization as a science is to discover the multiplicity of points of view and search for techniques to bridge or crosswalk them, an approach that came to be known in part as interoperability. More recently, Mai (2010) has told the story of the modern period in knowledge organization in more detail, tracing the search for realism in applicability of universal structures for knowledge and its order. Mai also makes reference to an important distinction that arose in the postmodern era of knowledge organization between classifications that are nascent or "naïve" (Beghtol, 2004, 19), which are the product of emergent scholarly activity in its observational (and hence nascent, prehypothetical) stage, and those that are "professional information-retrieval" orderings designed to facilitate discovery and retrieval of previously recorded knowledge elements. The natural consequence of the shift toward postmodern epistemological approaches and the acknowledgment of the naïve-professional dichotomy is the need for domain analysis, a methodological paradigm for the discovery of a knowledge base in a given, specific community.

The papers that now are seen as catalytical in knowledge organization came from Hjørland and Albrechtsen (1995) and were originally oriented to the information science community. Their 1995 paper suggested domain analysis as a programmatic approach or "new horizon" for information science (p. 400), "to study the knowledge domains as thought or discourse communities, which are part of society's division of labor." They suggested that components of knowledge organization were "reflections of the objects of the work" of discourse communities, incorporating even the criteria of individual community members. Domain analysis for the determination of system requirements as an aspect of computer science had found its way into information science as a means of orienting systems for information retrieval based on the specific requirements or information needs of research communities. The subtle shift from system requirements to discovery, recording, and tracking of a discourse community's ontology, or knowledge base was seen as a means of formalizing research for KOSs as a paradigmatic aspect of information science. Principle methods for domain analysis in information science, primarily informatics, were evolving from studies of communication among scientists into approaches to the mapping of disciplines and their evolution, particularly their paradigmatic evolution. A follow-on article (Hjørland and Albrechtsen, 1999) appeared in *Knowledge Organization* and was focused directly toward the KO community identifying domain analysis as a trend in classification research. In this paper, the pair wrote about the role of disciplines in modern KO research, the rise of inter- and multidisciplinarity, and the epistemological distinctions between scientific and bibliographic classifications (or, between taxonomy and typology of scientific disciplines, and classification of documents as it is known in information science). A consequence of pragmatic epistemology, they suggested, was the shift in knowledge organization (which they see as a component of information science) toward classification of knowledge in historical, social, and cultural contexts. Another consequence of pragmatic epistemology is to move away from the rationalist approaches to facet analysis that seeks to find universally applicable dimensions of knowledge, and to move toward non documentary-based or inter textuality-based approaches—empirical approaches—to the discovery of knowledge structures. In other words, although they do not say so explicitly in this paper, a shift is seen as evolving toward domain-analytical approaches to the discovery of domain-centric ontologies and to domain-epistemic orders of knowledge.

A 2002 paper from Hjørland (2002) lays out 11 formal techniques—he calls them approaches—to domain analysis for information science, now defined as methodological means for shifting information science away from universal approaches to information retrieval and toward a multiplicity and interplay of information activities in specialist communities. Specialist communities range from new subdisciplines to work-based environments and eventually to any community with a literature, a common goal or role, and a common information need. The 11 techniques, which are analyzed in detail in later chapters of this book, range from subject pathfinders to specialized classifications, from informetric to epistemological studies, and from genre analyses to documentation of heuristics for artificial information. Hjørland (2003) writes about the fundamental components of knowledge organization as a science, articulating two critical aspects of a postmodern theory (although he does not use that term), which are an emphasis on activity theory, and a distinction among epistemological approaches that are by necessity based in communities of discourse. The focus on discourse communities is a natural consequence of reliance on activity theory, because it sees knowledge as the product of the activity of discourse. In this manner, all activity can be seen as knowledge producing, and all knowledge produced can be seen as the product of activity, with the primary epistemological focus on the discourse responsible for knowledge production.

1.3 Domain analysis formulated as a paradigm for knowledge organization

Finally in 2003, in an introduction to a special issue of *Knowledge Organization* on domain analysis as an approach to information science, Hjørland and Hartel (2003) focus attention on the emergence of domain analysis as a paradigm in knowledge organization (although they do not use those words), in particular, acknowledging criticism from the information science community that the techniques have been too focused on scholarship apart from other human endeavor and that there have been too few case studies to demonstrate appropriate methodologies. Eight formal papers in the special issue push the boundaries of domain analysis, then, by extending the techniques outside of scholarly communities, by presenting clear case studies of analyses of specific and specifically bounded domains, and by expressing domain analysis pointedly as a methodology for knowledge organization.

It is Tennis' (2003) paper in the special issue that defines two axes for the functioning of domain analysis as a methodological paradigm for the discovery of transferable analytical ontology, in other words as a methodological paradigm for knowledge organization specifically. The two axes are extension and intension. The terms mean breadth and depth, respectively, and come from (2003, p. 192) "areas of modulation," and explicit name and inclusion–exclusion parameters, and "degrees of specialization," which can include focus and intersection. In the ensuing years, nearly 100 studies that can be characterized as domain analytical have been conducted in the domain of knowledge organization; those studies, which have fully demonstrated a wide variety of methods covering an equally diverse group of domains are analyzed in Chapter 2 of this book. Almost all of those studies trace their origin, or their paradigmatic allegiance, to Hjørland's catalytical work.

At the 2010 International Society for Knowledge Organization (ISKO) International Conference in Rome, Roberto Poli conducted a workshop on domain theory connected to the notion of levels of reality, a still emerging paradigm in knowledge organization. The idea of levels of reality is modeled on biological imperatives such that cells constitute organisms, which are living entities, which are biological entities, and so forth. Rather than a hierarchy of mutual exclusivity genus–species relationships, levels of reality are incorporated both from top-down and bottom-up. Thus, a domain theory based on the idea of levels of reality suggests analysis of domains at different levels posing different requirements for knowledge discovery. Poli suggests that domains can be defined by their "natural boundaries" (p. 146). Domains that are "categorically closed" require a different framework from those lower levels which they incorporate. Another principal (p. 147) is "maximal partition of reality" meaning that the domain includes all "entities selected by its categorical framework." We can see easily here an echo of Tennis' notions of two axes for domain analysis—extension and intension. Extension parallels the natural boundaries of a categorically closed domain, and intension defines the entities selected for inclusion in a bounded domain's categorical framework.

Poli also proposes two facets to define the "dimensions" of domain analysis (pp. 148–149), which he summarizes in a table (Table 1.1). We could draw several parallels from this table to components of knowledge organization. We could see "items" as parallel to "concepts" or "phenomena," which can be analyzed from various epistemic stances. Poli's work is not widely cited in the domain-analytical studies that follow it chronologically, but it shows how the larger domain of knowledge organization has embraced the domain-analytical paradigm, which has begun to mature and evolve. In the next chapter, we will review nearly 100 domain-analytical studies conducted in the KO domain, with the purpose of informing KO and KOSs, since the catalytical papers by Hjørland and his colleagues.

Table 1.1 **Facet groups (Poli, 2010, p. 150)**

Item	Name
Analysis	Kind
	Ambit structure property matter
Process	Internal process
	Operation patient function outcome
	By-product agent
Context	Context
Space time	Space time

The remainder of this book is devoted to techniques for conducting empirical domain-analytical studies for the purpose of advancing knowledge organization. The theoretical base is the idea of a postmodern knowledge universe in which many realities or dimensions may coexist and in which interoperability requires understanding each domain fully. We understand a domain to be a group with a common knowledge base that engages in discourse. The study of the group's discourse is the most basic empirical tool we have in our quiver. Our tools range from ethnographic participant observations to critical theoretical analysis of discourse in documents, to metrical extraction of terms and thematic plotting based on the trace evidence of citations, and to the simple mapping of thematic clusters. These are the tools of postmodern domain analysis, for the fueling of a multiverse of interoperable discourse.

Above I posited a very simple definition of a domain. Here is the definition I posed in 2012 based on an epistemological analysis of most of the studies conducted in KO to that point in time (p. 114):

A domain is best understood as a unit of analysis for the construction of a KOS. That is, a domain is a group with an ontological base that reveals an underlying teleology, a set of common hypotheses, epistemological consensus on methodological approaches, and social semantics. If, after the conduct of systematic analysis, no consensus on these points emerges, then neither intension nor extension can be defined, and the group thus does not constitute a domain.

To unpack the definition is to comprehend the methodological requirements of domain analysis. Within the science of knowledge organization, a domain is a group that requires or generates its own system for knowledge organization. A domain, therefore, has to be a group with a common understanding of its knowledge base, and in order for that to happen the group has to have a common goal for its existence. A primary school faculty has education of its charges as its common goal. It might also have cultural continuity as a goal. Both of those goals constitute underlying teleology that shapes the knowledge base shared by the community. A knowledge base is seen in this way as the evolutionary product of the activity, or work, of the group in question. The shared knowledge base, or ontology, of the community should emerge from analysis of their common vocabulary, either in their everyday speech or in their writings. A domain engaged in activity will exhibit a set of common methodological approaches to its work. That is, it will go about its work in a specific way or set of ways that are agreed to as appropriate by and for the entire group. A primary school faculty has perhaps a curriculum and set of teaching methods as its methodological platform; these typically are based in documents and real experience, suggesting a blend of pragmatism and empiricism as primary epistemological points of view, but of course historicism will be present wherever cultural objectives are primary. Evidence of their epistemological consensus should emerge from analysis of the documents with which they work. Social semantics means that the group shares meaning in and through its discourse and this will be true wherever there is visible analyzable discourse.

Scholarly communities ranging from entire disciplines—like knowledge organization itself—to individual departments—such as, for example, the Knowledge Organization Research Group at the University of Wisconsin, Milwaukee—are generally the targets of domain analysis. Such communities tend to be highly productive in terms of creating and disseminating knowledge in documents or other recordable evidentiary artifacts. They also tend to recognize each others' work through citing practice or some form of referencing controlled by the community. In Gladwell (2013), itself a domain analysis of people and ideas who win from positions of strength that are perceived to be positions of weakness, the story of early impressionists figures prominently: we learn that Cézanne, Degas, Monet, Pissaro, Renoir, and Sisley succeed by avoiding altogether the formal venue of Parisian "Salon" painting, placing their work instead in an exhibition of little contemporary note of their own making and on their own terms (White and White, 1992); essentially determining not to be lost in the bulk of the normal distribution of contemporary Parisian art of their day. The distinction gave them notoriety, which led to their success. Rather than allowing their works to be lost among the bulk of properly referenced acceptable work, they gained advantage by deliberately populating a segment of the long tail. Their works, therefore, were singularly referenced and thereby gained notoriety. The meaning of their work, impressionist, was determined by their own closed domain and not imposed from the larger culture. They were in essence an emerging domain, but with a clear common ontology, teleological goal, epistemological approach, and social semantics. (In the hundred or so papers analyzed in the next chapter of this book there are no domain analyses of art communities, *per se*, although artists produce a rich body of artifactual evidence of their discourse, verbal, and nonverbal, and their exhibits usually are documented in some way that could be used as one approach to domain analysis.)

The story of the Impressionists (at least told in this way) is reminiscent of the many small, potentially emergent domains of application within the metadata community told by Beak and Smiraglia (2014). These clusters are sufficiently small that their productivity does not rise into the upper tier of major themes in studies of the Dublin Core Metadata Initiative community, yet they persist from year to year and are visible in what was termed the "granularity" of the larger domain's intension. Another example, from the knowledge organization domain, is the nascent community devoted to ethics in knowledge organization, which has had two productive conferences (Smiraglia, 2014a, 2015). The small "Milwaukee Conferences on Ethics" provide venues in which this otherwise granular theme can itself evolve into a domain. Although domain analysis itself is still a nascent methodological paradigm in knowledge organization, domain analysis can be used to reveal the contours of these nested and interrelated conceptual components of knowledge-producing domains.

At some level all domain-analytical research is focused on finding the concepts at the core of each domain's ontology. It is these concepts that are the core elements of knowledge that can be organized, and it is these concepts, however realized or defined, that provide the intellectual platform for either common KOSs or interoperable systems. The search for the concept, then, is the primary objective of domain-analytical research in the larger science of knowledge organization. This is what distinguishes our research from similar studies in the fields of information, sociology, or computer science.

1.4   Domain analysis is metatheoretical

Research in domain analysis can be said to be metatheoretical, meaning that it incorporates many theoretical poles at once, and deliberately so, in order to provide methodological triangulation as a means of construct validity. That is, most of the techniques applied to domain analysis are qualitative to some degree, and results are often limited by the sources available for analysis. Therefore, it becomes important to analyze the domain from different points of view, or different theoretical poles, to see whether results overlap or coincide or yield a confusing mix of conceptual positions. As part of the catalytical work in the special issue of *Knowledge Organization* in 2003 Hjørland and Hartel wrote that domains are constituted of ontological dimensions, and epistemological and sociological concepts (p. 44): "domains are dynamic," as they play a symbiotic role in the evolution of a community's knowledge base and the real world perception of it. Our KO research group is functioning as workers in an educational workspace, even at the same time that it occupies the intellectual space of the larger domain of knowledge organization as a science. Our primary school faculty functions as a working unit in an educational and cultural workspace, even as it borrows cultural knowledge from all parts of society but gleans its working knowledge from the community of primary education. Our impressionist painters occupy a leading research front in the history of art, conceptually and artistically, even as they comprise the sole residents of their own specialized artistic front. It is the interactions of the ontological, epistemological, and sociological priorities that define a domain's work as productive activity and thus reveals its critical role both in the evolution of knowledge and in the comprehension of knowledge as a scientific entity.

As we will see in Chapter 2 ahead, the majority of approaches to domain analysis are empirical and involve the analysis of artifactual evidence, usually in the form of documents and their contents. A primary form of domain analysis is what I have called informetric, meaning metrical techniques applied to data from the source documents of a domain. Elsewhere, distinctions are made among bibliometric, cybermetric, scientometric, and informetric research (Cronin and Sugimoto, 2015). For our purposes, I will use the term informetric to cover all such cases. Most arise from bibliometric techniques discovered as part of the analysis of citations as trace evidence for the evolution of ideas. The remainder of this book will focus precisely on these empirical methods for domain analysis because these are the most promising tools for the construction of ontologies of known conceptual elements in scholarly discourse.

1.4.1 Bibliometric theory in domain analysis

Bibliometric analysis has a long history. Much of the intellectual basis for statistical bibliography emerged from the documentation movement and so has roots in thinking by Otlet (1934). Some of the earliest demonstrable theoretical positions are those of Bradford and Lotka, and these are described in Di Bellis (2009). Much of our ability to engage in bibliometric research comes from the legacy of Eugene Garfield, who founded the Institute for Scientific Information, which has become the Web of Science/Web of Knowledge. In information science, the key authors who have mapped both the utility and the techniques of bibliometric research are White and McCain (see for example White and McCain, 1989), although much recent theoretical work and historical documentation have emerged from Cronin and Sugimoto (e.g., 2014, 2015). Bibliometric studies seek to quantify in replicable terms processes of scholarly discourse, based on the trace evidence of citation patterns. They are based on theoretical distributions that have been observed at a metalevel in all of science. A simple straightforward explanation of most of the material that follows can be found in Pao (1989, pp. 13–39). The description here is presented as a form of overview of the metatheoretical aspect of domain analysis in knowledge organization.

Bibliometric research arose from studies of communication within scholarly communities in a variety of contexts, which are heavily dependent on documents as evidence of both formal and informal communication patterns and networks. Formal forms of communication are those represented by peer-reviewed publications such as journals, conference papers, and monographs; available documentary evidence is dependent on the community. Scientific communities generate journal articles and conference papers that are, in turn, indexed by commercial concerns such as Thomson Reuters or Elsevier, whose *Web of Science* and *Scopus*, respectively, databases supply easily accessible and analyzable citation data. Citations made by scholars in their peer-reviewed works are a form of trace evidence of thematic or theoretical relationships, and these can be used to generate visualizations of thematic or theoretical paradigms within specific communities. In some applied scientific communities technical reports serve a similar communicative purpose. In nonscientific domains, other forms of documentation must be relied upon to analyze communication within the domain. Other scholarly communities, such as those in the social sciences and humanities, also can be analyzed by using their citations as trace evidence of thematic and theoretical relationships, but because citation practices are different, citation-based profiles differ along several theoretical continua. In nonscholarly communities, analysis must be based on whatever documentary trace evidence is available or on nondocumentary analyses such as ethnographic studies.

Obsolescence is the rate at which ideas (themes, theories) pass out of favor and seem to disappear from the literature. Immediacy, its semantic opposite is the usually seemingly exponential rate at which current or very recent research is cited. Immediacy is a sign of a research front; obsolescence is usually a sign of what is called "absorption," meaning that once results from a specific article are absorbed into the theoretical framework of the paradigm it ceases to be cited as newer, more immediate works are cited instead. Price's (1963) statistical analysis of the then exponential growth of scientific literature from 1660 to 1960 yielded several theoretical observations that led to techniques for the quantification of immediacy and obsolescence. For instance, we can calculate a "half-life" as a measure of obsolescence. Bibliometric half-life depends on the metaphor of half-life in physics, in which the term is a measurement of the time required for half of the atoms of a radioactive substance to disintegrate. In domain analysis, bibliometric half-life tells us the periodicity of use of individual cited documents. That is, half-life is the period of time during which half of the total number of citations to a specific document were made. In general, the shorter half-life identifies domains with rapid obsolescence, which usually also means rapid absorption of research results into the domain's canon. There is wide variability among domains, especially on the trajectory from the pure sciences to the humanities. Price created an index PI for Price's Index, or the percentage of citations to literature that were 5 or fewer years older than the citing article. PI was used, then, to delineate domains according to "hardness" (or "softness," also often used). "Hard sciences" are domains anchored in methodological rigor, usually in the form of controlled experimental research. But the term also is a proposal of classical sciences such as physics, chemistry, and natural sciences. Scientific disciplines were said to range from hard (PI $\geq 42\%$) to soft ($33 \geq PI \geq 22\%$), to technical literature (PI $\leq 21\%$). In general, from Price's work, we can take the following (see Di Bellis, 2009, p. 66): "half [of the papers cited] referred to a ... tightly defined subset of earlier literature; ... the most cited papers were also more recent than the rest." This tight and relatively immediate cluster may be taken as one indication of an active research front in a domain. In other words, by analyzing the quantitative indicators of immediacy and obsolescence, we can make one approach to defining a research front, in a domain where a tightly knit heavily cited cluster is visible. Also, comparative measures of immediacy and obsolescence help to visualize the differences or similarities among domains.

Journals are the formal venues for most scholarly communication, and studying them as whole works is also one means of identifying productive elements of a research front. Of course, few journals are devoted to topical areas that are as narrowly defined as most domains under study. For exampe, even in the field of knowledge organization, the principle journal *Knowledge Organization* is devoted to the entire field. Thus it would likely be the most cited journal in all domains within KO, but there are no journals devoted to specific narrow aspects of KO, such as "integrative levels," "multilingual thesauri," or "ethics in KO." Bradford's (1948) study of the productivity of scientific journals led to the discovery of what we now call a "power-law," that illustrates a geometrically progressed region of productivity in a frequency distribution of journal productivity. Bradford's law can be seen in a frequency distribution of journal productivity arranged in the order of decreasing numbers of articles on a given subject. There will be a nucleus of periodicals more particularly devoted to the subject and several groups or zones containing the same number of articles as the nucleus, when the numbers of periodicals in the nucleus and succeeding zones will be as n:n2:n3... (Bradford, 1948).

Here is an example from the 2012 12th International ISKO Conference, Mysore, India. This is from a frequency distribution of all of the journals cited in the conference's 55 contributed papers (Table 1.2).

Table 1.2 Journal productivity in 2012 ISKO proceedings

Knowledge Organization	33
Journal of the American Society for Information Science	21
Journal of Documentation	17
Information Studies	9
Archivaria, 35(Spring): 24–37	5
Information Processing and Management, 24(5): 513–523	5
Cataloging & Classification Quarterly, 37(1/2): 33–47	4
Ciência da Informação (Impresso), 37: 60–75	4
Scire, 1(1): 149–157	4
Journal of Information Science, 34: 651–66	3
Library Trends	3
Revista Ibero-americana de Ciência da Informação, 1: 77–99	3
SRELS Journal of Information Management, 42(4): 361–382	3
Bulletin des Bibliothèques de France	2
Cognitive Psychology, 7(4): 573–605	2
Knowledge Engineering Review, 11(2)	2
Library Resources & Technical Services, 38: 27–46	2
Webology, 2(4): Article 19	2
ACM SIGSOFT Software Engineering Notes	1
American Archivist	1
Análisis documental de contenido de textos literarios narrativos...	1
Argus	1
Bulletin of the American Society for Information Science and Technology	1
Culture del testo e del document, 9(25): 5–25	1
Development, 32(1): 1–25	1
DGZ, Rio de Janeiro, 7(3): 1–18	1
Expert Systems with Application, 11(4): 519–529	1
IEEE Transactions on Visualization and Computer Graphics, 14(2): 1–12	1
IFLA SET Bulletin, 9(1): 33–35	1
Online Information Review	1

Table 1.2 **Continued**

Organizational Behavior and Human Performance, 1: 3–30	1
Information Standards Quarterly, 23(1): 20–26	1
Intelligent Systems, 14(1): 37–46	1
International Classification, 8(2): 86–91	1
Journal of Computer-Mediated Communication, 8(4)	1
Journal of Digital Information, Available: http://journals	1
Journal of Verbal Learning and Verbal Behavior, 21(1): 1–20	1
Journal of Web Semantics, 6(3): 203–217	1
Knowledge Acquisition, v	1
Language in Society, 2: 45–80	1
LIBER Quarterly: The Journal of European Research Libraries	1
Library Science with a Slant to Documentation	1
Multilingual thesaurl for modern world	1
Organización del Conocimiento en Sistemas de Información y Documentación	1
Perspectiva em Ciência da informação	1
Redes de leitura e Ciência da Informação, Informare	1
Revista da Escola de biblioteconomia da UFMG	1
Revue d'informatique et de recherche opérationnelle	1
Transnational Associations	1
Visual Resources Association Bulletin	1
Archival Science	1
Journal of Knowledge Management	1
Journal of the Society of Archivists	1

The reader will perhaps notice that this table comes from a raw data file. Notice that there is a long tail of journals with only a single publication. Because I know this list normally would be jettisoned (or, at least not reproduced for publication), it has not been edited carefully. There are 34 journals in this list of singletons, so this constitutes region 3. The second region begins at *Journal of Information Science* and has 23 articles in 9 journals. We will jettison that too. The top region, also has 9 journals, but this time these 9 journals contain 112 articles, or slightly more than 3 times the number in the lower region. Still, the topmost region of the table shows us the specific journals from which the science presented at the conference was drawn, and arguably their relative influence.

Author productivity is frequently a bibliometric measure that can help identify both research fronts and invisible colleges. As we have seen, a research front is the leading edge of a domain in which most of the current work at any point in time is taking place. We have seen that immediacy is a characteristic of a research front, and that most of its publications will appear in a small cluster of influential venues. We also can visualize a research front by mapping citations, especially by identifying authors and their individual productivity. We know from Lotka's inverse square law of scientific productivity (Lotka, 1926) that the total number of authors in a given subject publishing prolifically are in a fixed ratio to the number authors producing only one contribution. Interestingly, Lotka's law holds in almost all domains in some observable fashion. The small cluster of prolific authors are those whose work will usually persist over time; all the rest are quickly absorbed or ignored and become obsolete.

Research fronts are defined by the nucleus in any given field. Often research fronts are populated by scientists who make up what Crane (1972) called "invisible colleges." These are groups of scholars who work in specific theoretical paradigms. Often only the tip of the iceberg of their work appears in print; much of what they do is invisible because they spend time together in meetings or conversing online or even comparing notes over cocktails. However, domain-analytical techniques such as author cocitation analysis often can reveal the outlines of working invisible colleges. Author cocitation analysis is a visualization process in which citations in a domain are tracked by co-occurrence as a similarity measure, which happens when papers are cited together. If linked pairs identified by cocitation are numerous, they likely represent a perceived similarity either topical or theoretical shared by the cocited papers. More importantly, the perception of similarity leading to cocitation is a means of visualizing the knowledge base of a research community. That is, authors writing in a domain that is thriving use their citations to link their work to acknowledged thematic groups, topical clusters, or theoretical paradigms existing within their domain. Author cocitation analysis, then, allows a visualization of key clusters within a domain. The technique was introduced by White and Griffith (1981) and reviewed in detail in White and McCain (1997). Two influential examples are White and McCain's (1998) analysis of information science, and by extension (although not an author cocitation analysis *per se*), White's (2001) use of citation theory to analyze the individual citation identities of authors. McCain (2009) introduced a process called tricitation, in which she attempts to raise the citation profile of an individual author over time by interpreting the contexts of cocitation.

1.4.1.1 Instantiation

Instantiation is the term applied to the phenomenon of multiple realization of information objects over time (Smiraglia, 2008). More specifically, the term is used to describe the phenomenon in which (p. 6): "multiple iterations of information content are extant." The simplest examples are works that exist in several subsequent editions, or works for which many translations are available. Research has demonstrated two essential types of instantiation termed derivations and mutations. The difference is that between a copy of a work, in which none of the intellectual content has changed, and instantiations, in which the intellectual content has been altered in some way. Intellectual content can be ideational and semantic; that is, the ideas represented in a work are transmitted in some way that conveys their meaning. Derivations are instantiations in which there is little change in ideational content with some degree of change in semantic content; the work is said to have been derived from its predecessors over time. Mutations are instantiations in which there is quite a lot of change in ideational content, and thus also in semantic content; the work has actually mutated into what could be considered, essentially, a new work. Written texts with multiple subsequent editions are considered to be kinds of derivations, because the ideational content has been updated over time. Translations of works are arguably considered to be mutations, because although an attempt is made to retain ideational content, the act of representing the content in a different language will cause subtle shifts in the ideas along cultural linguistic lines. Of course, a translation has completely different semantic content. More complex examples exist among works that have been reinterpreted for multiple uses over time, such as stories that are used to generate screenplays, which become movies, from which novelizations, musical sound recordings, and even lunch boxes and action characters are spun off. In such complex examples, each point at which the ideational content changes is considered a node, a new related work, and each node can have its own branching set of instantiations. Figure 1.1 is a visual representation of a complex instantiation network.

The terms and concepts identified here relating to instantiation are developed further in Smiraglia (2002b, 2006, 2008); most of the empirical research quantifying instantiation among information objects is reviewed in Smiraglia (2001, 2002a).

The phenomenon of instantiation is well known in bibliographic circles and is the basis of the entity–relationship model enshrined in the *Functional Requirements for Bibliographic Records* (FRBR, 1998). Research also has demonstrated the role of instantiation among archival and artifactual entities (Smiraglia, 2004), among scientific models (Coleman, 2002) and among records of evolutionary biologists (Greenberg, 2009). The more recent object-oriented *FRBRoo* (v.2.0, 2013) incorporates empirical understanding into a revised representation of bibliographic instantiation, such that it can be fully compatible with the cultural heritage ontology known as CIDOC-Conceptual Reference Model or CRM (v. 5.0.4, 2011).

The study of instantiation is in a nascent stage. Few domains have been fully analyzed although there has been one detailed study of instantiation among musical documents by Vellucci (1997), and there were two smaller scale studies of theological literature (Smiraglia, 2002c) and American literature (Marchese, 2002). The phenomenon is known to follow a power-law distribution (Smiraglia, 2008, p. 11) such that

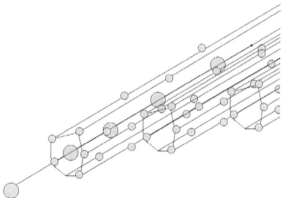

Figure 1.1 Instantiation networks nested within nodes (Smiraglia, 2008, p. 26).

most works exist in only one instantiation, but large instantiation networks, though rare, occur among less than one-third of the works in a given domain. Although popularity of works was suspected to be involved in the process of instantiation this hypothesis was not demonstrated (Smiraglia, 2007), and instead the catalyst for instantiation seems to be some form of canonicity. Age of the progenitor works is associated with the size and complexity of instantiation networks, such that older progenitors have more derivative instantiations, but more recent progenitors have more mutation instantiations. Bibliometric studies of domains often reveal classically cited works by prolific authors, and these works (or, the output of these authors) represent the region of large instantiation networks in many domains. Recently it has been suggested that instantiation could be added as a dimensional facet to concept-based classifications (Smiraglia and van den Heuvel, 2013). The technique for identifying and quantifying instantiation networks will be described in Chapter 4.

1.4.2   Critical theory, semiotics, and discourse analysis

Domain analysis as a methodological paradigm for knowledge organization has tended to be incorporated into the general epistemological framework of the field, which is to say that there is a clear trajectory in published domain analysis between works that are empirical and those that follow more humanistic approaches, generally rational or historical (Smiraglia, 2012b). In the preceding section, I discussed briefly some empirical approaches to bibliometrics that have been found to be useful in domain analysis for KO. The other large class of theoretical approaches fall under the rubric of what is termed "critical theory." Critical theory analyses can be used to reveal social and cultural influences. Arising originally in sociology and literary theory, the techniques have been used successfully if intermittently in information science and also in knowledge organization. Among influential authors in the application of critical theory to problems in domain analysis for KO are Habermas (1984) and Foucault (1972); semiotic applications frequently reference both Saussure (1959) and Peirce (1991). A 2010 book by Leckie, Given, and Buschman presents an overview of applications in information science. The application of critical theory will not be discussed further in this book.

Discourse analysis has proved a popular methodology for knowledge organization domain analysis. The use of discourse analysis applied to problems in information science was demonstrated by Frohmann (1992, 1994) and Budd and Raber (1996). Of course, any conversation may be considered a form of discourse, and narrative analysis of it, such as is used in ethnographic research, can reveal subtle contextual contours. Frohmann (1994, p. 120) wrote: "Discourse analysis takes discourse as its object of analysis. Its data is talk; not what the talk refers to but the talk itself." Frohmann placed discourse analysis as a research method in information science as analogous to other qualitative methodologies. The classical theory of symbolic interactionism was described by Blumer (1969) and is the umbrella concept underlying qualitative methods. The theory is based on the notion that humans interact symbolically, and that the symbols implicit in human interaction effect perception. Perception, of course, effects context, and the concepts that are the atomic entity of KOSs are always subject to contextual interpretation. Thus, discourse analysis is one means of revealing the interacting symbolic contexts in the discourse that are affecting perception. But extending the discourse metaphor even further for domain analysis means selecting key elements of discourse in a domain. These may range from published articles or monographs to individual utterances and a whole range of knowledge elements in between. So discourse analysis rests in the first instance on the selection of sources, their function as representative of discourse, and their relationship to the domain under analysis. Budd and Raber (1996, p. 218) address the concept of "the object of examination in discourse analysis" in some detail and focus on the notion that in communication both form and function are critical. With reference to both Habermas (1984) and Foucault (1972) they conclude (p. 225): "An ultimate goal of discourse analysis is to place a particular body of writing or speech in theoretical frameworks of communication and discourse." Drawing on Foucault (1972) and his own prior (1994) work, Frohmann set out with some precision a framework for the use of discourse analysis (2001, p. 18):

> *The kinds of practices at issue are those that: 1) bring about the existence of statements and sets of statements; 2) inscribe statements in specific document forms; and 3) establish and legitimate platforms of enunciation, whereby certain statements and certain documents become stabilized and gain authority. Discourse analysis also draws our attention to 4) the intersections and relationships of these practices and their institutional settings, with other, non-documentary practices and institutional settings; and 5) the political, economic, and cultural institutions that configure practices with documents.*

Analysis of discourse has often been used in knowledge organization to reveal underlying epistemic stances in KOSs (Olson, 1996). Discourse analysis is an important tool for domain analysis for the richness of context it can reveal in the blending of conceptual and social constructs within and among domains.

1.5   Domain analysis is a multimethod paradigm

Just as domain analysis for knowledge organization has incorporated many theoretical perspectives, so has it been demonstrated to be a multimethod paradigm. Many of the methods employed, even those that are empirical, are enhanced by the sort of methodological triangulation recommended in qualitative paradigms. We saw above at least three different ways to quantify a research front—usually a definitive indication of the presence of a research front in any domain involves the use of all the three and those together with other techniques for visualization, such as coword analysis. Critical theory employs a brace of analytical techniques, to provide multiple trajectories for analysis. Frequently in knowledge organization discourse analysis is accompanied by one or more empirical analyses as well, to provide a multitheoretical, multimethods perspective.

References

Beak, J., Smiraglia, R.P., 2014. Contours of knowledge: core and granularity in the evolution of the DCMI domain. In: Babik, W. (Ed.), Knowledge Organization in the 21st Century: Between Historical Patterns and Future Prospects: Proceedings of the Thirteenth International ISKO Conference 19–22 May 2014, Kraków, Poland. In: Advances in Knowledge Organization, vol. 14. Ergon Verlag, Würzburg, pp. 136–143.

Beghtol, C., 2004. Naïve classification systems and the global information society. In: McIlwaine, I.C. (Ed.), Knowledge Organization and the Global Information Society; Proceedings of the Eighth International ISKO Conference, 13–16 July, London, UK. In: Advances in Knowledge Organization, vol. 9. Ergon Verlag, Würzburg, pp. 19–22.

Blumer, H., 1969. Symbolic Interactionism: Perspective and Method. University of California Press, Berkeley.

Bradford, S.C., 1948. Documentation. Crosby Lockwood, London.

Budd, J.M., Raber, D., 1996. Discourse analysis: method and application in the study of information. Inform. Process. Manag. 32, 217–226.

CIDOC Conceptual Reference Model, 2011. Produced by the ICOM/CIDOC Documentation Standards Group, continued by the CIDOC CRM Special Interest Group, version 5.0.4. http://www.cidoc-crm.org/official_release_cidoc.html.

Coleman, A.S., 2002. Scientific models as works. Catalog. Classif. Quart. 33 (3/4), 129–159.

Crane, D., 1972. Invisible Colleges: Diffusion of Knowledge in Scientific Communities. University of Chicago Press, Chicago.

Cronin, B., Sugimoto, C., 2014. Beyond Bibliometrics: Harnessing Multidimensional Indicators of Scholarly Impact. MIT Press, Cambridge, MA.

Cronin, B., Sugimoto, C., 2015. Scholarly Metrics Under the Microscope: From Citation Analysis to Academic Auditing. Information Today, Medford, NJ.

Dahlberg, I., 2006. Knowledge organization: a new science? Knowl. Organ. 33, 11–19.

Di Bellis, N., 2009. Bibliometrics and Citation Analysis: From the Science Citation Index to Cybermetr. Scarecrow, Lanham, MD.

Foucault, M., 1972. The Archeology of Knowledge and the Discourse on Language. Pantheon, New York.

FRBRoo, 2013. Bekiari, C., Doerr, M., Le Boeuf, P., Riva, P. (Eds.), Object-Oriented Definition and Mapping from *FRBRer*, *FRAD* and *FRSAD* Version 2.0. http://www.cidoc-crm.org/frbr_drafts.html.

Frohmann, B., 1992. The power of images: a discourse analysis of the cognitive viewpoint. J. Doc. 48, 365–386.

Frohmann, B., 1994. Discourse analysis as a research method in library and information science. Libr. Inf. Sci. Res. 16, 119–138.

Functional Requirements for Bibliographic Entities, 1998. Final Report, approved by the Standing Committee of the IFLA Cataloguing Section on September 1997 as amended and corrected through February 2009. http://www.ifla.org/files/cataloguing/frbr/frbr_2008.pdf.

Gladwell, M., 2013. David and Goliath: Underdogs, Misfits, and the Art of Battling Giants. Little, Brown, New York.

Greenberg, J., 2009. Theoretical considerations of lifecycle modeling: an analysis of the Dryad Repository demonstrating automatic metadata propagation, inheritance, and value system adoption. Catalog. Classif. Quart. 47 (3), 380–402.

Habermas, J., 1984. The theory of communicative action, vol. 1, Reason and the Rationalization of Society (T. McCarthy, Trans.). Beacon Press, Boston.

Hjørland, B., 2002. Domain analysis in information science: eleven approaches, traditional as well as innovative. J. Doc. 58, 422–462.

Hjørland, B., 2003. Fundamentals of knowledge organization. Knowl. Organ. 30, 87–111.

Hjørland, B., 2009. Concept theory. J. Am. Soc. Inf. Sci. Technol. 60, 1519–1536.

Hjørland, B., Albrechtsen, H., 1995. Toward a new horizon in information science: domain analysis. J. Am. Soc. Inf. Sci. 46, 400–425.

Hjørland, B., Albrechtsen, H., 1999. An analysis of some trends in classification research. Knowl. Organ. 26, 131–139.

Hjørland, B., Hartel, J., 2003. Introduction to a special issue of *Knowledge Organization*. Knowl. Organ. 30, 125–127.

Lotka, A.J., 1926. The frequency distribution of scientific productivity. J. Wash. Acad. Sci. 16, 317–323.

Mai, J.-E., 1999. A post-modern theory of knowledge organization. In: Woods, L. (Ed.), Proceedings of the 62nd annual meeting of the American Society for Information Science. Information Today, Medford, NJ, pp. 547–556.

Mai, J.-E., 2010. The modernity of classification. J. Doc. 67, 710–730.

Marchese, C., 2002. Works of American literature. Unpublished seminar paper. Long Island University.

McCain, K., 2009. Using tricitation to dissect the citation image: Conrad Hal Waddington and the rise of evolutionary developmental biology. J. Am. Soc. Inf. Sci. Technol. 60, 1301–1319.

Olson, H.A., 1996. Dewey thinks therefore he is: the epistemic stance of Dewey and *DDC*. In: Green, R. (Ed.), Knowledge, Organization and Change: Proceedings of the Fourth International ISKO Conference, 15–18 July 1996. INDEKS Verlag, Frankfurt/Main, pp. 302–312.

Otlet, P., 1934. Traité de documentation: le livre sur le livre, théorie et pratique. Editiones Mundaneum, Bruxelles.

Pao, M.L., 1989. Concepts of Information Retrieval. Libraries Unlt., Englewood, CO.

Peirce, C.S., 1991. Hoopes, J. (Ed.), Peirce on Signs: Writings on Semiotic. Indiana University Press, Bloomington.

Poli, R., 2010. Workshop on levels of reality as a KO paradigm: domain theory, a preliminary proposal. In: Gnoli, C., Mazzochi, F. (Eds.), Paradigms and Conceptual Systems in Knowledge Organization, Proceedings of the 11th International ISKO Conference, 23–26 February 2010, Rome, Italy. In: Advances in Knowledge Organization, vol. 12. Ergon Verlag, Würzburg, pp. 145–151.

Price, D.J.S., 1963. Little Science, Big Science. Columbia University Press, New York.

de Saussure, F., 1959. in collaboration with A. Riedlinger; trans., with an introd. and notes by W. BaskinBally, C., Sechehaye, A. (Eds.), Course in General Linguistics. McGraw-Hill, New York.

Smiraglia, R.P., 2001. The Nature of a Work: Implications for the Organization of Knowledge. Scarecrow Press, Lanham, MD.

Smiraglia, R.P. (Ed.), 2002a. Works as Entities for Information Retrieval. Haworth Information Press, New York.

Smiraglia, R.P., 2002b. Works as signs, symbols, and canons: the epistemology of the work. Knowl. Organ. 28, 192–202.

Smiraglia, R.P., 2002c. Bridget's *Revelations*, William of Ockham's *Tractatus*, and *Doctrine and Covenants*: qualitative analysis and epistemological perspectives on theological works. Catalog. Classif. Quart. 40 (3–4), 225–251.

Smiraglia, R.P., 2004. Knowledge sharing and content genealogy: extending the "works" model as a metaphor for non-documentary artifacts with case studies of Etruscan artifacts. In: McIlwaine, I. (Ed.), Knowledge Organization and the Global Information Society; Proceedings of the Eighth International ISKO Conference, 13–16 July, London, UK. In: Advances in Knowledge Organization, vol. 9. Ergon Verlag, Würzburg, pp. 309–314.

Smiraglia, R.P., 2006. Empiricism as the basis for metadata categorization: expanding the case for instantiation with archival documents. In: Budin, G., Swertz, C., Mitgutsch, K. (Eds.), Knowledge Organization and the Global Learning Society: Proceedings of the 9th ISKO International Conference, Vienna, 4–7 July 2006. In: Advances in Knowledge Organization, vol. 10. Ergon Verlag, Würzburg, pp. 383–388.

Smiraglia, R.P., 2007. The "works" phenomenon and best selling books. Catalog. Classif. Quart. 44 (3–4), 179–195.

Smiraglia, R.P., 2008. A meta-analysis of instantiation as a phenomenon of information objects. Culture del testo e del documento 9 (25), 5–25.

Smiraglia, R.P., 2012a. Epistemology of domain analysis. In: Smiraglia, R.P., Lee, H. (Eds.), Cultural Frames of Knowledge. Ergon, Würzburg, pp. 111–124.

Smiraglia, R.P., 2012b. Universes, dimensions, domains, intensions and extensions: knowledge organization for the 21st century. In: Neelameghan, A., Raghavan, K.S. (Eds.), Categories, Contexts, and Relations in Knowledge Organization: Proceedings of the Twelfth International ISKO Conference, 6–9 August 2012, Mysore, India. In: Advances in Knowledge Organization, vol. 13. Ergon Verlag, Würzburg, pp. 1–7.

Smiraglia, R.P., 2014. The Elements of Knowledge Organization. Springer, New York.

Smiraglia, R.P., 2015. Ethics in knowledge organization: two conferences point to a new core in the domain. Encontros bibli 20 (1), 1–17.

Smiraglia, R.P., van den Heuvel, C., 2013. Classifications and concepts: towards an elementary theory of knowledge interaction. J. Doc. 69, 360–383.

Tennis, J.T., 2003. Two axes of domains for domain analysis. Knowl. Organ. 30, 191–195.

Vellucci, S.L., 1997. Bibliographic Relationships in Music Catalogs. Scarecrow Press, Lanham, MD.

White, H.D., 2001. Authors as citers over time. J. Am. Soc. Inf. Sci. Technol. 52, 87–108.

White, H.D., Griffith, B.C., 1981. Author co-citation: a literature measure of intellectual structure. J. Am. Soc. Inf. Sci. 32, 163–171.

White, H.D., McCain, K.W., 1998. Visualizing a discipline: an author co-citation analysis of information science. 1972-1995. J. Am. Soc. Inf. Sci. 49, 327–355.

White, H.D., McCain, K., 1989. Bibliometrics. Annu. Rev. Inform. Sci. Technol. 24, 119–186.

White, H.D., McCain, K., 1997. Visualization of literatures. Annu. Rev. Inform. Sci. Technol. 32, 99–168.

White, H., White, C., 1992. Canvases and Careers; Institutional Change in the French Painting World, with a New Foreword and a New Afterword, University of Chicago Press ed. University of Chicago Press, Chicago.

Domain analysis as a methodological paradigm in knowledge organization

2.1 A methodological paradigm in KO

Domain analysis is one methodological paradigm within the science of knowledge organization. In domain analysis, the purpose is to reveal the contours of held knowledge, whether that be in the form of live discourse or recorded documentation, by analyzing the elements of specific communities who share a common ontology, or knowledge base. The objectives of domain analysis are to map and visualize the intellectual parameters of shared knowledge in a given community, such that results can be put to use in knowledge organization systems for the furtherance of the community's own discourse and for its intellectual contributions at large. Put simply, our purpose is to visualize the concepts shared by a group that works together, to discern the working vocabulary that defines those concepts, and to map the relationships among the concepts. Domain analysis is one aspect of knowledge organization where both ontology and epistemology come together; we want to see which concepts constitute the knowledge base, or ontology, of discourse in a community, but we also want to see how those concepts are used and understood.

Domain analysis as a named, purposive methodological paradigm in knowledge organization can be dated from Hjørland's catalyzing paper in 2002; although the roots go back further to the understanding that knowledge organization had come to a domain-centric postmodern viewpoint (Mai, 1999). Rather than seeking universally applicable rules for formulating a single ontology, postmodern KO seeks to reveal the ontological parameters of each specific community, choosing instead to search for techniques for interoperability to allow cross-domain communication. Domain analysis as a methodological paradigm, then, has two demands. The first is that each domain be analyzed exhaustively and continuously. The second is that to facilitate theory building, there must be replicated and continuous analysis both of specific domains and of their multiplicity of domains together. That is, it is imperative that knowledge organization as a science turn its metaphorical microscope to look at every possible domain from the workplace to the neighborhood to the household to the academic disciplines and beyond. As marching orders for a new science the turn to domain analysis has meant that more KO scholars are needed to analyze more domains. But it also has meant that more analyses of already analyzed domains also are required.

In the 12 years or so in which KO has turned its attention specifically in a domain-analytical direction, there has been a modest increase in the number and frequency of studies specifically devoted to using Hjørland's 11 approaches to the analysis of domains for the purpose of revealing their shared ontologies. In this chapter, we look briefly at those studies, which appear in KO's three principal venues. Interestingly, we know from research (Smiraglia, 2011, 2012, 2013a) that those venues are primarily the biennial international conference proceedings from the International Society for Knowledge Organization (published in the series *Advances in Knowledge Organization*) and the journal *Knowledge Organization*, and a smattering of papers from the information science literature at large. Other sources are doctoral dissertations produced in schools of KO, although most of these are eventually reported formally in one of the other three venues.

2.2 Domain-analytical literature from the KO domain

Domain analysis has been explicitly a critical aspect of the knowledge organization domain since Hjørland's charge to the community in 2002. The evolution of empirical methods can be observed in the literature of the domain, which is found predominantly in the proceedings of international ISKO conferences and in the journal *Knowledge Organization*. In this section I review, briefly, studies from those venues as well as from some doctoral dissertations. The point of this curt review is to point readers to specific examples of the application of specific methods.

2.2.1 International ISKO conference proceedings

Forty-one domain-analytical papers from ISKO International conferences were sorted methodologically for this review. That is, each paper was categorized using 1 of the 11 approaches to domain analysis from Hjørland's list. Interestingly, only 7 of the 11 approaches have been used in papers in the proceedings. Most often used are terminological or informetric studies, and discourse analyses. Obviously, bibliometrical studies constitute the most used forms of domain analysis in published knowledge organization research. One could hazard a guess that this is because the written and indexed record is so plentiful. But it is important to note that many aspects of knowledge organization and the domains studied are not indexed by the most prominent indexing services. This means that much of the work must be done manually, which is time and labor intensive, but also involves much cleaning of data, usually in the form of poorly or inconsistently formatted citations. Interestingly 33 definable domains have been analyzed in ISKO conference papers since 2002, ranging from archival science to transport engineering. Only two domains have been visited more than once; there were two studies of gender studies, and eight studies of the aspects of knowledge organization. The domain-analytical lens has been turned inward more often than outward it would seem. Papers in these clusters are reported here and reports within each cluster are chronological.

2.2.1.1   Producing literature guides or subject gateways

Coleman (2004) used content maps and pathfinder networks to test the domain vocabulary of engineering novices. Madalli et al. (2014) drew on a variety of known KOSs for music to generate a faceted ontological representation.

2.2.1.2   Empirical user studies

Campbell (2004) conducted a qualitative study of gay and lesbian information users to detect the value of facet analysis for generating flexible and adapatable approaches to browsing systems. Pajarillo (2006) conducted an ethnographic study of home health care nurses, using diaries, participant observation, focus groups, and questionnaires. Loehrlein (2008) used content analysis of a corpus of records management texts to discover Wittgensteinian form-of-life contexts. Participants subsequently ranked interpretations of the texts based on complexity judgments. Sanatjoo (2010) used a mixed-methods work-task-oriented methodology (WOM) to develop a thesaurus for a plant pathology academic unit. Actors, tasks, and information behaviors were identified, conceptualized, and subjected to facet analysis. This methodology is similar to, but not quite coextensive with Cognitive Work Analysis (CWA). Orrico et al. (2012) used a case study of researchers in transport engineering together with content analyses of artists' manifestos to extract a theoretical model of the use of metaphors. Frâncu and Popescu (2014) combined content analysis and interviews with traditional bibliometric measures to develop a profile of the cultural shift in the evolution of Romanian knowledge organization resulting from a 20-year period during which applied research continued in libraries while theoretical work was discontinued in academic institutions.

2.2.1.3   Bibliometrical studies

López-Huertas (2006) studied Spanish-language gender studies in Uruguayan publications selecting terms from titles, abstracts, and main headings in monographs, articles, and reports, and section or column headings in specialized periodicals. Chaomei et al. (2008) used bibliographic records from the *Web of Science*™ (WoS)™ to look for culture and geographic identity in the domain of astronomy surrounding the Sloan Digital Sky Survey. Three text-mining systems were used for the analysis, utilizing author keywords and noun phrases extracted from titles and abstracts. Comparisons were made across geopolitical boundaries. Tanaka (2010) used citation, author co-citation, and co-word analyses to delineate the domain of computational science; she worked with records from the Brookhaven National Labs to identify a set of core authors in this multidisciplinary domain, then used traditional *WoS* sources. Smiraglia (2012) used citation, author co-citation, and co-word analyses to analyze trends in the dimensions of knowledge organization research. Guimarães et al. (2012) used a form of content analysis to extract theoretical references from articles in the journal *Knowledge Organization*. Guimarães and Tennis (2012) used citation analysis to visualize the presence of indexing theory in ISKO proceedings to date. Arboit et al. (2012) similarly used citation analysis to identify the most prolific authors in ISKO proceedings from 2002 to 2010, and then to classify their papers using a knowledge organization-specific schema. A form of social network analysis was employed, using the classification to create a network map among the prolific authors. The objective was to reveal the most influential thematic categories in the domain. Deokattey et al. (2012) used co-word and facet analysis to conceptualize a domain ontology in the field of Test Blanket Modules, a cluster within thermonuclear fusion. Indexer-assigned descriptors were downloaded from the International Nuclear Information System (INIS) database. Co-word clusters were subjected to facet analysis, and results were used to generate concept maps of the domain. Neelameghan and Raghavan (2014) cast a domain-analytic net over the concept of the science of consciousness, or the domain of paranormal phenomena, by generating a frame of essential works from three bibliographic sources, and then analyzing the subject headings in bibliographic records for those works to visualize the domain. Raghavan and Ravichandra Rao (2014) used tools from the WoS to frame and visualize the domain of facet analysis. Graf and Smiraglia (2014) continued a series of papers based on domain analysis of the evolution of the *Encyclopedia of Milwaukee*. Beak and Smiraglia (2014) also continued a research stream investigating the granularity of the Dublin Core Metadata Initiative.

2.2.1.4   Document and genre studies

Rafferty (2010) reported a study in which she used genre theory to analyze a qualitatively constructed frame of genre novels, as a prelude to developing a knowledge organization system for affective dimension indexing. Plot synopses were developed and then filtered by plot types, ideological stances, modality markers, etc.

2.2.1.5   Epistemological and critical studies

Furner and Dunbar (2004) applied Critical Race theory to the treatment of mixed race in the *Dewey Decimal Classification*. Lima et al. (2008) modeled the domain of legal resources, in particular their diachronic evolution, using the object-oriented version of the *FRBR* model. López-Huertas and López-Perez (2010) used literature review to generate epistemological analyses of KO and psychiatry in order to reveal the contours of discourse and epistemological behavior in each. García-Marco et al. (2010) generated a model of the domain of narrative fiction using genre analysis, narratology, and facet analysis. Alexiev and Marksbury (2010) studied the epistemological bases of the domains of knowledge organization and terminology to visualize their similarities of purpose and evolutionary trajectory.

2.2.1.6   Terminological studies, language for special purpose, database semantics, and discourse studies

López-Huertas et al. (2004) used four specialized thesauri in gender studies to map terminological conceptual structures. Miller et al. (2006) extracted terms from listserv archives to analyze the terminology of the domain of education for knowledge organization. Lin et al. (2006) used a visual-concept-explorer application applied to terms extracted from PubMed to analyze the terminology in the domain of Influenza virus

A-avian. Mustafa El Hadi (2008) used discourse community analysis for the paradoxical comparison of sense and nonsense in a corpus of texts related to the Darfur political and humanitarian crisis with the specific context of conflict early warning. Barros and de Moraes (2010) used discourse analysis applied to key manuals of archival science to extract key concepts of description and classification. Zherebchevsky (2010) used terminological analysis to examine the presence of formalism in the discourse of the 10th International ISKO Conference held in Montréal in 2008. Kwaśnik and Flaherty (2010) analyzed autism as a domain by using traditional terms from *Medical Subject Headings (MeSH)* mapped with terms extracted from WebMD. Gontijo et al. (2012) applied discourse analysis to Brazilian e-government documents as a means of generating an ontological representation for public policy. Guimarães et al. (2014) applied content analysis to papers selected from the entire run of ISKO proceedings to generate conceptual parameters, or the extent, of the domain of knowledge organization. Dodebei and Orrico (2014) mapped the domain of social memory by using conceptual analyses of syllabi and key texts. Campbell (2014) used facet analysis applied to protocols for dementia care.

2.2.1.7 Scientific cognition, expert knowledge, and artificial intelligence

Ou et al. (2004) applied automatic discourse parsing to sociology dissertation abstracts as a means of sentence categorization. Ibekwe-SanJuan and SanJuan (2010) applied an automatic topic mapping system to *WoS* records of KO publications 1998–2008—predominantly journal articles and conference papers; they used term extraction to create topic visualization.

2.2.2 Knowledge Organization, *the journal of ISKO*

Since Hjørland's call for greater focus on domain analysis, and possibly as a result of a postmodern domain-specific thrust in the KO community, the majority of articles in ISKO's journal *Knowledge Organization*, have been reports of domain-analytical research. In 2011 the journal increased in size and frequency from quarterly to bimonthly, and a lengthy bibliography section was moved from the journal to online publication as a database, making more space for research. As a consequence, the number of domain-analytical research articles increased over the period under analysis. In 2003 a double issue of *Knowledge Organization*, guest edited by Hjørland and Hartel (2003a,b) included seven original domain-analytical papers. A total of 33 domain-analytical articles are sorted here by methodological cluster and date.

2.2.2.1 Producing literature guides or subject gateways

Vinod Kumar and Nikam (2014) analyzed a glossary and a thesaurus to generate a web portal for the yogic science domain in India.

2.2.2.2 Constructing special classifications and thesauri

Manzi (2009) describes the development of a specialized classification for philosophy at the Scuola Normale Superiore, Pisa, Italy. Deokattey et al. (2010) used mixed methods including content analysis, facet analysis, and clustering to develop a proto-type ontology for the domain of accelerator driven systems. Campos et al. (2013) used both quantitative and qualitative analyses of gene terminology from formal bioinformatics ontologies in the domain of trypanosomatides.

2.2.2.3 Empirical user studies

Albrechtsen and Pejtersen (2003) introduced CWA as a domain-analytical method and applied it to the analysis of national film research archives. Gazan (2003) employed qualitative methods—observation, narrative analysis, semistructured interviews, and a think-aloud protocol—to the problem of developing metadata for an environmental information system. Hartel (2003) conducted a case study (using a set of amalgamated techniques) on the hobby of cooking; the theoretical background for the paper contains an epistemological analysis of serious leisure to locate the domain of hobbies. Chaudhry and Ling (2005) used a work-based qualitative method to review and recreate a taxonomy for a business consulting firm. Chiu (2005) conducted a case study of the library and information service industry in Taiwan, using semistructured participant interviews and narrative and content analyses. Munk and Mørk (2007) conducted an empirical study of tagging communities using content analysis of a random sample of tags from *Delicious.com*. Marchese and Smiraglia (2013) reported the use of CWA in a human resources consultancy to generate an emergent taxonomy demonstrating pivot terminology, or border objects for professional-client communication. Ménard and Dorey (2014) used empirical user analysis to evaluate a bilingual taxonomy for image indexing. Youlin et al. (2014) used empirical analysis of a Chinese information science database to project the evolution of an onto-thesaurus. Zemmels (2014) reported a qualitative analysis of laptop users to uncover everyday practices of media engagement.

2.2.2.4 Bibliometrical studies

Freitas et al. (2012) used bibliometrical analysis to make approximations between author productivity in knowledge organization in Brazil. De la Moneda Corrochano et al. (2013) returned to bibliometric analysis of Spanish research in knowledge organization for the period 2002–2010. Oikarinen and Kortelainen (2013) used bibliometrical analysis of a catalog of archeological artifacts from Jakobstad, Finland. Smiraglia (2013b) used bibliometric analyses including citation analysis, co-word analysis, and author co-citation analysis to analyze the coherence of the set of researchers writing about *Functional Requirements for Bibliographic Records* (*FRBR*) and its family of conceptual models. Meireles et al. (2014) used bibliometric analyses of the domain of artificial neural networks. Kenyon (2014) used bibliometric analyses to describe the impact of research as a domain, across the humanities, social sciences, and the arts. Weller (2014) used informetric analysis to describe the impact of Twitter research in social science. Zhao and Wu (2014) used network analysis to analyze information science in China.

2.2.2.5 Historical studies

Keilty (2009) used historical analysis of knowledge surrounding queer phenomena, or the domain of homosexuality. Souza et al. (2012) used historical analysis to develop a proposal for a multidimensional taxonomy of KOSs. Couzinet (2012) used historical analysis of key knowledge organization documents to generate an analysis of the domain of French KO researchers. Ribeiro (2014) used historical and epistemological analysis of Portuguese language archival literature to generate a set of dimensions for the use of classification in archives.

2.2.2.6 Document and genre studies

Abrahamsen (2003) used a sequence of genre and epistemological analysis to describe KOSs for music, especially those used in libraries, especially with regard to the treatment of popular musical genres.

2.2.2.7 Epistemological and critical studies

Sundin (2003) applied epistemological analysis tools to the journal literature of the Swedish nursing profession. Zins and Guttman (2003) combined epistemological analyses in a four-phase qualitative study of the literature of social work to create a knowledge map. Furner (2007) expanded his use of Critical Race theory to analyze race-related categories in the *Dewey Decimal Classification*. Kaipainen and Hautamäki (2011) used epistemological analysis of the information systems domain to suggest the potential of multiperspective KOSs.

2.2.2.8 Terminological studies, language for special purpose, database semantics, and discourse studies

Ørom (2003) brought discourse analysis to the literature of the arts, with a special focus on the visual arts in exhibitions. Christensen (2008) analyzed segments of *LCSH* and LCC for term usage in the domain of gays and lesbians. Ibekwe-SanJuan (2008) expanded her discourse analysis of astronomy researchers with a case study of the Sloan Digital Sky Survey. Scaturro (2013) analyzed controlled vocabularies and faceted taxonomies in the domain of a performing arts digital library. Pinto, Rabelo, and Girão (2014) analyzed patient records to evaluate the specialized thesaurus SNOMED-CT.

2.2.3 Domain-analytical papers from the information science literature

Domain-analytical techniques, most of them originally bibliometric or informetric in nature, were pioneered in the domain of information science for the purpose of understanding communication among scholars, the evolution of literatures, and by extension the effect of these on the problems of information retrieval. In fact, it was to the information science community that Hjørland's first paper calling for domain analysis as a new method was addressed. Work in this vein is methodologically complex in information science. However, few of these papers report research designed to elicit the knowledge bases of domains for use in knowledge organization. A small number of such papers, published in a variety of journals, are described in this narrative. Only 7 of the 11 proposed approaches have been used in this research.

2.2.3.1   Producing literature guides or subject gateways

Estevão and Strauhs (2013) used survey research and content analysis to propose the contours of a reference ontology for the domain of historical organizational memory. Klavans and Boyack (2011) used *Scopus* data to generate comparative global maps of the domains of information science and computer science, for use as target-literature gateways.

2.2.3.2   Constructing special classifications and thesauri

Tian et al. (2013) used an extraction tool and word-split software to gather feature word groups from patent abstracts. The word groups, formalized by control words, were used to construct a domain KOS. Arencibia-Jorge et al. (2007) used content analysis and bibliometric methods to construct a domain ontology called a "conceptual structure" for the domain of benign prostatic hyperplasia.

2.2.3.3   Empirical user studies

Huang (2013) tested the use of a generic function-based typology in the analysis of clinical questions. Hartel (2010) used ethnographic techniques, including interviews, and structured participant observation to study the domain of home gourmet hobby cooking.

2.2.3.4   Bibliometrical studies

Guimarães et al. (2012) used bibliometrical methods to analyze the contents of the Spanish knowledge organization and representation journal *SCIRE*, to categorize domain interactions among information science, knowledge organization, indexing, cataloging, and document analysis. Smiraglia (2013a,b,c) used bibliometric, co-word, and author co-citation analyses to analyze the influence of the works of S.R. Ranganathan on the field of knowledge organization over time. Beghtol used term extraction and co-word analysis to generate a domain-analytical ontology for fiction studies from the *MLA Bibliography*. Lee et al. (2010) used co-word analysis of terms extracted from the LISA database to develop a cluster model of the digital libraries domain. Miguel et al. (2008) used category co-citation analysis of publications associated with two museums to generate domain profiles. Moya-Anegón et al. (2008) used categories *Web of Science Journal Citation Reports* to compare domain structures of scientific domains by extracting all records including "Spain" or "France" or "England" and then looking or category co-citation. The results are meta-analytical. Nascimento and Marteleto (2008) analyzed the internal structure and corpus of a journal *Revista Pampulha* to generate the information structure of a professional (not academic) discourse community.

2.2.3.5 Epistemological and critical studies

Lam (2011) creates an epistemological analysis of key documents in the knowledge organization of musicianship as discovered in music education.

2.2.3.6 Terminological studies, language for special purpose, database semantics, and discourse studies

Pattuelli and Rubinow (2013) analyzed the semantic constructs in DBpedia within the domain of jazz to reveal the contours of diverse approaches to domain knowledge in the Linked Open Data dataset. Dutta et al. (2011) used terms extracted from a corpus of research articles in physics to generate comparative cluster analyses of Brane theory and Fermi Liquid. Jeong and Kim (2010) used co-word analysis of terms extracted from calls for papers and conference programs in biomedical informatics; terms were compared with terms from the formal *MeSH* thesaurus.

2.2.4 Smiraglia CAIS and NASKO papers and KO editorials

I have written several domain-analytical papers, some in series, as experimental work. Most have been published in conference proceedings or as editorials in *Knowledge Organization*, but have not (yet) been compiled into journal contributions. In general, my approach has been incremental to observe evolution of domains and to generate journal articles only when meta-analytical results seem appropriate for reporting (e.g., see Smiraglia (2011, 2012, 2013a) which is a summary of many studies of ISKO as a domain.) Apologias aside, most of this have been reported either at conferences of the Canadian Association for Information Science (CAIS), at successive North American Symposia on Knowledge Organization (NASKO), or as editorials in *Knowledge Organization*. Inspired by White's 2003 paper about "authors as citers" I attempted to demonstrate the influence of Patrick Wilson's seminal *Two Kinds of Power*, a book that had influenced my own research immensely. The result Smiraglia (2007) was an analysis of 77 seminal papers in which co-word analysis was used to visualize thematic streams, and author co-citation analysis was used to visualize perceived similarity among the authors. The two methods often are used together to provide methodological triangulation, presenting either confirming or conflicting thematic results that emerge from the visualizations. A similar approach, added to citation analyses from the *Web of Science*™ was used to suggest dimensions of the influence of Ranganathan in Smiraglia (2013a,b,c) reported above. The consideration of the influence of classic authors as domain markers should be taken up in a more deliberate manner in every domain under analysis in order to explain the perceptive role of classic, if outlier, authors in domain visualizations.

These same empirical techniques applied to conference proceedings were used to track the evolution of the music information retrieval (MIR) movement, from its inception as the International Symposium on MIR in 2000 to its maturation and concretization as the International Society for MIR in 2009 (Smiraglia, 2006; 2009a). Similarly, with Jihee Beak, two studies have described the nascent Dublin Core metadata community (Beak and Smiraglia, 2014 above, and Beak and Smiraglia, 2013).

Tracking the evolution of KO as a domain has become a part of my role as editor of *Knowledge Organization*. In these studies, I use these same domain-analytic techniques to generate quick visualizations of themes and co-citation among authors at regional or international KO conferences. Formal results have been reported in Smiraglia (2009b, 2011) and summarized in Smiraglia (2013a,b,c) reported above.

2.3 Visualizing domain analysis as a methodological paradigm

Hjørland's 11 approaches have been fully implemented in the knowledge organization domain. Nearly a 100 studies have been conducted and reported in the domain's formal literature and summarized here. What we have seen is that the majority of analytical studies use empirical methods such as informetric or terminological techniques, but large numbers of discourse analyses, genre analyses, and epistemological analyses also are attempted. Fewer critical studies and historical analyses have been generated, but some are represented. Construction of pathfinders and subject gateways are rarely reported in the formal literature of the domain, but are the active work of applied knowledge organization. Figure 2.1 is a simple visualization of the numbers of published studies by venue over time.

What we can see in Figure 2.1 is the growth of the domain analysis paradigm in knowledge organization over time, from Beghtol's (1995) study of fiction (which coincided chronologically with Hjørland and Albrechtsen's paper on domain analysis for information science), and a concommitant steady increase from the point of Hjørland's (2002) call for more domain analysis in KO. This visualization also demonstrates the diatonic relationship between research in *AIKO* and *KO*—between conference proceedings and the domain's formal journal. At both ends of the period, roughly equal numbers of studies appeared in both venues; in between the majority of studies appeared in proceedings. There also has been growth in the total amount of domain-analytical research over the whole period. Respectable numbers of KO domain-analytical papers were appearing in information science journals by 2011. The paradigm has gained a foothold in KO.

Figure 2.2 shows the distribution of the studies among Hjørland's 11 approaches over time and across the three formal venues described above. The visualization makes it immediately clear that the majority of studies appear in conference proceedings, and also, as noted above, that the majority of studies are informetric or terminological or report domain-specific KOSs. But we also can see that most of the

Number of articles by venue by year

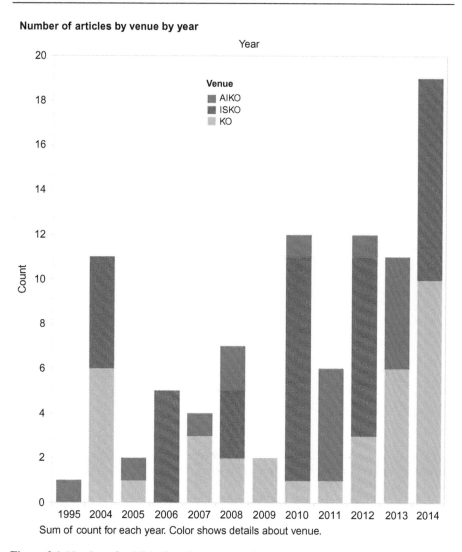

Figure 2.1 Number of published studies by venue by year.

approaches are populated to some extent. Figure 2.3 is a more detailed and colorful representation of the same data.

This visualization shows the greater variety in use of the 11 approaches in studies reported in proceedings. Another way to articulate this result is to say there are more empirical studies in the formal *KO* journal. We also can see that there is a steady if slow increase in the number of KO domain-analytical papers across time, even in general information science journals. This is a sign of the influence of the paradigm extending outside the bounds of KO as a domain.

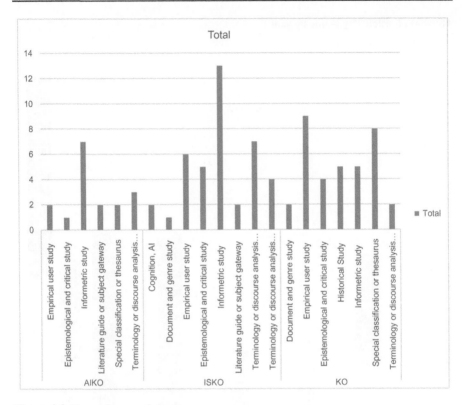

Figure 2.2 Type of approach by venue.

We also can see that the "taxonomy," as it were, of domain-analytical approaches, can now be revised in light of research experience. These approaches are barely used:

- Special classification, indexing specialty, historical study, and scientific communication do not occur in *AIKO*.
- Literature guide, indexing specialty, genre study, and scientific communication do not occur in *KO*.
- Indexing specialty, historical study, genre study, discourse analysis, scientific communication, and cognition/artificial intelligence do not appear in information science venues.

As well, critical theory appears only twice. It is possible that these results are artifacts of the present analysis. Hartel (2003, 233) suggested domain analysis could be viewed as a kind of collectivist metatheoretical approach, which, among other things, means more than one approach can be combined in any particular study. This would, of course, impair the assignment of studies to individual approaches, or obscure approaches used as secondary or triangulating methods. In other words, some of the approaches in the bulleted list above might, in fact, have been used in combination in some of the reported studies. This is clearly the case with historical and genre studies. That caveat aside, it would seem that the KO community has little interest in

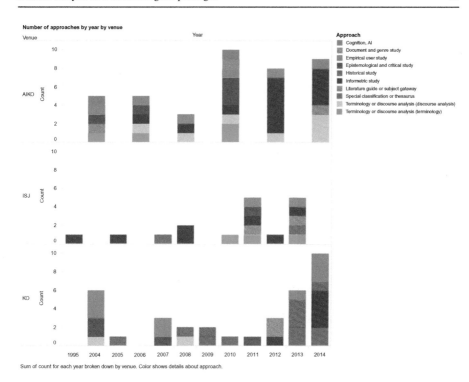

Figure 2.3 Approaches by year by venue.

pursuing scientific communication studies as domain analytical, leaving that method instead to the general information science community. Similarly, indexing and retrieving specialties remain isolated from the KO and information science domains, reported instead in the literature of the specialized domains, as Hjørland (2002) noted (429). Finally, it is clear from the present analysis that terminological studies and discourse analyses can be broken out into their own individual categories. Database semantics appeared a few times in the present analysis, and could also constitute its own category. These latter represent subtle shifts in the intension of the domain-analytical paradigm in KO.

Finally, a wide variety of domains have been analyzed in these studies. These 30 domains have each been studied once:

Accelerator driven systems
Architecture
Artificial neural networks
Artists
Autism
Benign prostatic hyperplasia
Biomedical informatics
Brazil public policy
Business consulting firm

Computational science
Darfur crisis
Dementia care
Engineering novices
Evidence-based clinical medicine
Genre novels
Historical organizational memory
HR firm
Influenza A-avian
Information science and computer science
Information science
Laptop users
Legal resources
Narrative fiction
Natural science museums
Paranormal phenomena
Patent abstracts
Patient records
Philosophy at Scuola Normae Superiore Pisa
Plant pathologists
Portuguese language archives
Records managers
Social memory
Social science research
Social work
Sociology dissertations
Transport engineering
Visual arts in exhibitions
Yogic science

Another eight domains have been studied twice:

Astronomy
Cooking
Chinese information science
Digital libraries
Dublin Core Metadata Initiative
Encyclopedia of Milwaukee
Gender studies
Nursing
Race
Tripsanomatides

and four more three times:

Archives
Image searching
LGBT
Physics
Social media

There are 4 studies of music and 22 studies of aspects of knowledge organization. We will look closely at the theoretical implications of the breadth of this list of domains in the final chapter of this book. For now, the list is shown here to indicate the ongoing success of the postmodern paradigm of domain-specific domain-analytical research in knowledge organization.

References

Abrahamsen, K.T., 2003. Indexing of musical genres: an epistemological perspective. Knowl. Organ. 30, 144–169.

Albrechtsen, H., Pejtersen, A.M., 2003. Cognitive work analysis and work centered design of classification schemes. Knowl. Organ. 30, 213–227.

Alexiev, B., Marksbury, N., 2010. Terminology as organized knowledge. In: Gnoli, C., Mazzochi, F. (Eds.), Paradigms and Conceptual Systems in Knowledge Organization, Proceedings of the 11th International ISKO Conference, 23–26 February 2010, Rome, Italy. In: Advances in Knowledge Organization, vol. 12. Ergon Verlag, Würzburg, pp. 363–370.

Arboit, A.E., Gracio, M.C.C., Oliveira, E.F.T.d., Bufrem, L.S., 2012. Relationship between authors and main subject categories in the knowledge organization domain: a bibliometric approach. In: Neelameghan, A., Raghavan, K.S. (Eds.), Categories, Contexts, and Relations in Knowledge Organization: Proceedings of the Twelfth International ISKO Conference, 6–9 August 2012, Mysore, India. In: Advances in Knowledge Organization, vol. 13. Ergon Verlag, Würzburg, pp. 44–50.

Arencibia-Jorge, R., Vega-Almeida, R.L., Martí-Lahera, Y., 2007. Domain analysis for the construction of a conceptual structure: a case study. LIBRES Res. Electron. J. 17 (2), 1–26.

Barros, T.H., de Moraes, J.B.E., 2010. From archives to archival science: elements for a discursive construction. In: Gnoli, C., Mazzochi, F. (Eds.), Paradigms and Conceptual Systems in Knowledge Organization, Proceedings of the 11th International ISKO Conference, 23–26 February 2010, Rome, Italy. In: Advances in Knowledge Organization, vol. 12. Ergon Verlag, Würzburg, pp. 398–404.

Beak, J., Smiraglia, R.P., 2013. With a focused intent: evolution of DCMI as a research community. In: Proceedings of the International Conference on Dublin Core and Metadata Applications, Lisbon, Portugal: DC-2013, pp. 126–134. http://dcpapers.dublincore.org/pubs.

Beak, J., Smiraglia, R.P., 2014. Contours of knowledge: core and granularity in the evolution of the DCMI domain. In: Babik, W. (Ed.), Knowledge Organization in the 21st Century: Between Historical Patterns and Future Prospects, Proceedings of the 13th International ISKO Conference, Krakow, Poland, 19–22 May 2014. In: Advances in Knowledge Organization, vol. 14. Ergon-Verlag, Würzburg, pp. 136–143.

Beghtol, C., 1995. Domain analysis, literary warrant, and consensus: the case of fiction studies. J. Am. Soc. Inf. Sci. 46, 30–44.

Campbell, G., 2004. A queer eye for the faceted guy: how a universal classification principle can be applied to a distinct subculture. In: McIlwaine, I.C. (Ed.), Knowledge Organization and the Global Information Society; Proceedings of the Eighth International ISKO Conference, 13–16 July, London, UK. In: Advances in Knowledge Organization, vol. 9. Ergon Verlag, Würzburg, pp. 109–113.

Campbell, D.G., 2014. The human life as warrant: a facet analysis of protocols for dealing with responsive behaviors in dementia patients. In: Babik, W. (Ed.), Knowledge Organization in the 21st Century: Between Historical Patterns and Future Prospects, Proceedings of the 13th International ISKO Conference, Krakow, Poland, 19–22 May 2014. In: Advances in Knowledge Organization, vol. 14. Ergon-Verlag, Würzburg, pp. 121–128.

Campos, M.L.d.A., Machado Campos, M.L., Dávila Alberto, M.R., Espanha Gomes, H., Linair Maria, C., de Lira e Oliveira, L., 2013. Information sciences methodological aspects applied to ontology reuse tools: a study based on genomic annotations in the domain of trypanosomatides. Knowl. Organ. 40, 50–61.

Chaomei, F.I.-S., Pinho, R., Zhang, J., 2008. The impact of the Sloan Digital Sky Survey on astronomical research: the role of culture, identity, and international collaboration. In: Arsenault, C., Tennis, J. (Eds.), Culture and Identity in Knowledge Organization: Proceedings of the 10th International ISKO Conference, Montréal, 5–8 August 2008. In: Advances in Knowledge Organization, vol. 11. Ergon Verlag, Würzburg, pp. 307–312.

Chaudhry, A.S., Ling, G.H., 2005. Building taxonomies using organizational resources: a case of business consulting environment. Knowl. Organ. 32, 25–46.

Chiu, T.-h., 2005. Attributes and factors affecting the organization of knowledge resources: a case study of the library and information service industry in Taiwan. Knowl. Organ. 32, 128–134.

Christensen, B., 2008. Minoritization vs. universalization: lesbianism and male homosexuality in *LCSH* and *LCC*. Knowl. Organ. 35, 229–238.

Coleman, A.S., 2004. Knowledge structures and the vocabulary of engineering novices. In: McIlwaine, I.C. (Ed.), Knowledge Organization and the Global Information Society; Proceedings of the Eighth International ISKO Conference, 13–16 July, London, UK. In: Advances in Knowledge Organization, vol. 9. Ergon Verlag, Würzburg, pp. 281–286.

Couzinet, V., 2012. Knowledge organization in information and communication sciences, a French exception? Knowl. Organ. 39, 259–267.

De la Moneda Corrochano, M., López-Huertas, M.J., Jiménez-Contreras, E., 2013. Spanish research in knowledge organization (2002–2010). Knowl. Organ. 40, 28–41.

de Moya-Anegón, F., Vargas-Quesada, B., Chinchilla-Rodriguez, Z., 2005. Domain analysis and information retrieval through the construction of heliocentric maps based on ISI-JCR category cocitation. Inform. Proc. Manag. 41, 1520–1533.

Deokattey, S., Neelameghan, A., Kumar, V., 2010. A method for developing a domain ontology: a case study for a multidisciplinary subject. Knowl. Organ. 37, 173–184.

Deokattey, S., Dixit, D.K., Bhanumurthy, K., 2012. Co-word and facet analysis as tools for conceptualization in ontologies: a preliminary study for a micro-domain. In: Neelameghan, A., Raghavan, K.S. (Eds.), Categories, Contexts, and Relations in Knowledge Organization: Proceedings of the Twelfth International ISKO Conference, 6–9 August 2012, Mysore, India. In: Advances in Knowledge Organization, vol. 13. Ergon Verlag, Würzburg, pp. 153–158.

Dodebei, V., Orrico, E.G.D., 2014. Knowledge in Social Memory: empirical experiment for a domain conceptual-discursive mapping. In: Babik, W. (Ed.), Knowledge Organization in the 21st Century: Between Historical Patterns and Future Prospects, Proceedings of the 13th International ISKO Conference, Krakow, Poland, 19–22 May 2014. In: Advances in Knowledge Organization, vol. 14. Ergon-Verlag, Würzburg, pp. 65–72.

Dutta, B., Majumder, K., Sen, B.K., 2011. Study of subject domain by keyword cluster analysis based on research articles: a case study from physics. Inform. Studies 17, 195–210.

Estevão, J.S.B., Strauhs, F.d.R., 2013. Proposta de uma ontologia como modelo de referência no domínio da Memória Organizacional Histórica (Portuguese). Perspectivas Em Ciencia Da Informacao 18 (4), 35–53.

Frâncu, V., Popescu, T., 2014. Twenty years after: scientific research in the field of knowledge organization in Romania (1993–2012). In: Babik, W. (Ed.), Knowledge Organization in the 21st Century: Between Historical Patterns and Future Prospects, Proceedings of the 13th International ISKO Conference, Krakow, Poland, 19–22 May 2014. In: Advances in Knowledge Organization, vol. 14. Ergon-Verlag, Würzburg, pp. 556–563.

Freitas, J.L., Junior, G., Faustino, R., Bufrem, L.S., 2012. Theoretical approximations between Brazilian and Spanish authors' production in the field of knowledge organization in the production of journals on information science in Brazil. Knowl. Organ. 39, 216–223.

Furner, J., 2007. Dewey deracialized: a critical race-theoretic perspective. Knowl. Organ. 34, 144–168.

Furner, J., Dunbar, A.W., 2004. The treatment of topics relating to peope of mixed race in bibliographic classification schemes: a critical race-theoretical approach. In: McIlwaine, I.C. (Ed.), Knowledge Organization and the Global Information Society; Proceedings of the Eighth International ISKO Conference, 13–16 July, London, UK. In: Advances in Knowledge Organization, vol. 9. Ergon Verlag, Würzburg, pp. 115–120.

García-Marco, F.-J., de Moraes, J.-B.-E., García-Marco, L.-F., Guimarães, J.-A.-C., 2010. Knowledge organization of fiction and narrative documents: a challenge in the age of the multimedia revolution. In: Gnoli, C., Mazzochi, F. (Eds.), Paradigms and Conceptual Systems in Knowledge Organization, Proceedings of the 11th International ISKO Conference, 23–26 February 2010, Rome, Italy. In: Advances in Knowledge Organization, vol. 12. Ergon Verlag, Würzburg, pp. 262–268.

Gazan, R., 2003. Metadata as a realm of translation: merging knowledge domains in the design of an environmental information system. Knowl. Organ. 30, 182–190.

Gontijo, M., Dodebei, V., Orrico, E., 2012. Discourse analysis as an approach to categorizing the domain of public policy: the case of Brazilian e-government. In: Neelameghan, A., Raghavan, K.S. (Eds.), Categories, Contexts, and Relations in Knowledge Organization: Proceedings of the Twelfth International ISKO Conference, 6–9 August 2012, Mysore, India. In: Advances in Knowledge Organization, vol. 13. Ergon Verlag, Würzburg, pp. 256–261.

Graf, A.M., Smiraglia, R.P., 2014. Race & ethnicity in the encyclopedia of Milwaukee: a case study in the use of domain analysis. In: Babik, W. (Ed.), Knowledge Organization in the 21st Century: Between Historical Patterns and Future Prospects, Proceedings of the 13th International ISKO Conference, Krakow, Poland, 19–22 May 2014. In: Advances in Knowledge Organization, vol. 14. Ergon-Verlag, Würzburg, pp. 114–120.

Guimaraes, J.A.C., Tennis, J.T., 2012. Constant pioneers: the citation frontiers of indexing theory in the ISKO international proceedings. In: Neelameghan, A., Raghavan, K.S. (Eds.), Categories, Contexts, and Relations in Knowledge Organization: Proceedings of the Twelfth International ISKO Conference, 6–9 August 2012, Mysore, India. In: Advances in Knowledge Organization, vol. 13. Ergon Verlag, Würzburg, pp. 39–43.

Guimarães, J.A., Pinho, F.A., Ferreira, G.M., 2012. Relações teóricas da organização do conhecimento com as abordagens de catalogação de assunto, indexação e análise documental: uma análise de domínio da revista Scire (1995–2010) (Portuguese). Scire 18 (2), 31–41.

Guimaraes, J.A.C., de Oliveira, E.T., Gracio, M.C.C., 2012. Theoretical referents in knowledge organization: a domain analysis of Knowledge Organization journal. In: Neelameghan, A., Raghavan, K.S. (Eds.), Categories, Contexts, and Relations in Knowledge Organization: Proceedings of the Twelfth International ISKO Conference, 6–9 August 2012, Mysore, India. In: Advances in Knowledge Organization, vol. 13. Ergon Verlag, Würzburg, pp. 31–38.

Guimarães, J.A., de Sales, R., Martínez-Ávila, D., Alencar, M.F., 2014. The conceptual dimension of knowledge organization in the ISKO proceedings domain: a Bardinian content analysis. In: Babik, W. (Ed.), Knowledge Organization in the 21st Century: Between Historical Patterns and Future Prospects, Proceedings of the 13th International ISKO Conference, Krakow, Poland, 19–22 May 2014. In: Advances in Knowledge Organization, vol. 14. Ergon-Verlag, Würzburg, pp. 101–106.

Hartel, J., 2003. The serious leisure frontier in library and information science: hobby domains. Knowl. Organ. 30, 228–238.

Hartel, J., 2010. Managing documents at home for serious leisure: a case study of the hobby of gourmet cooking. J. Doc. 66, 847–874.

Hjørland, B., 2002. Domain analysis in information science: eleven approaches—traditional as well as innovative. J. Doc. 58, 422–462.

Hjørland, B., Hartel, J., 2003a. Introduction to a special issue on domain analysis. Knowl. Organ. 30, 125–127.

Hjørland, B., Hartel, J., 2003b. Afterword: ontological, epistemological and sociological dimensions of domains. Knowl. Organ. 30, 239–245.

Huang, X., 2013. Applying a generic function-based topical relevance typology to structure clinical questions and answers. J. Am. Soc. Inform. Sci. Technol. 64 (1), 65–85.

Ibekwe-SanJuan, F., 2008. The impact of geographic location on the development of a specialty field: a case study of Sloan Digital Sky Survey in astronomy. Knowl. Organ. 35, 239–250.

Ibekwe-SanJuan, F., SanJuan, E., 2010. Knowledge organization research in the last two decades. In: Gnoli, C., Mazzochi, F. (Eds.), Paradigms and Conceptual Systems in Knowledge Organization, Proceedings of the 11th International ISKO Conference, 23–26 February 2010, Rome, Italy. In: Advances in Knowledge Organization, vol. 12. Ergon Verlag, Würzburg, pp. 115–121.

Jeong, S., Kim, H.-G., 2010. Intellectual structure of biomedical informatics reflected in scholarly events. Scientometrics 85, 541–551.

Kaipainen, M., Hautamäki, A., 2011. Epistemic pluralism and multi-perspective knowledge organization: explorative conceptualization of topical content domains. Knowl. Organ. 38, 503–514.

Keilty, P., 2009. Tabulating queer: space, perversion, and belonging. Knowl. Organ. 36, 240–248.

Kenyon, T., 2014. Defining and measuring research impact in the humanities, social sciences and creative arts in the digital age. Knowl. Organ. 41, 249–257.

Klavans, R., Boyack, K.W., 2011. Using global mapping to create more accurate document-level maps of research fields. J. Am. Soc. Inform. Sci. Technol. 62, 1–18.

Kwaśnik, B.H., Flaherty, M.G., 2010. Harmonizing profeesional and non-professional classifications for enhanced knowledge representation. In: Gnoli, C., Mazzochi, F. (Eds.), Paradigms and Conceptual Systems in Knowledge Organization, Proceedings of the 11th International ISKO Conference, 23–26 February 2010, Rome, Italy. In: Advances in Knowledge Organization, vol. 12. Ergon Verlag, Würzburg, pp. 229–235.

Lam, M., 2011. Towards a "musicianship model" for music knowledge organization. OCLC Syst. Serv. 27, 190–209.

Lee, J.Y., Kim, H., Kim, P., 2010. Domain analysis with text mining: analysis of digital library research trends using profiling methods. J. Inf. Sci. 36, 144–161.

Lima, J.A.d.O., Palmirani, M., Vitali, F., 2008. A time-aware ontology for legal resources. In: Arsenault, C., Tennis, J. (Eds.), Culture and identity in knowledge organization: Proceedings of the 10th International ISKO Conference, Montréal, 5–8 August 2008. In: Advances in Knowledge Organization, vol. 11. Ergon Verlag, Würzburg, pp. 63–69.

Lin, X., Aluker, S., Zhu, W., Zhang, F., 2006. Dynamic concept representation through a visual concept explorer. In: Budin, G., Swertz, C., Mitgutsch, K. (Eds.), Knowledge Organization and the Global Learning Society; Proceedings of the 9th ISKO International Conference, Vienna, 4–7 July 2006. In: Advances in Knowledge Organization, vol. 10. Ergon Verlag, Würzburg, pp. 367–374.

Loehrlein, A., 2008. The benefits of participating in a form of life: interpretations of complex concepts among experts and novices in records management. In: Arsenault, C., Tennis, J. (Eds.), Culture and Identity in Knowledge Organization: Proceedings of the 10th International ISKO Conference, Montréal, 5–8 August 2008. In: Advances in Knowledge Organization, vol. 11. Ergon Verlag, Würzburg.

López-Huertas, M.J., 2006. Thematic map of interdisciplinary domains based on their terminological representation. The Gender Studies. In: Budin, G., Swertz, C., Mitgutsch, K. (Eds.), Knowledge Organization and the Global Learning Society; Proceedings of the 9th ISKO International Conference, Vienna, 4–7 July 2006. In: Advances in Knowledge Organization, vol. 10. Ergon Verlag, Würzburg, pp. 331–338.

López-Huertas, M.J., López-Perez, M.J., 2010. Epistemological dynamics in scientific domains and their influence in knowledge organization. In: Gnoli, C., Mazzochi, F. (Eds.), Paradigms and Conceptual Systems in Knowledge Organization, Proceedings of the 11th International ISKO Conference, 23–26 February 2010, Rome, Italy. In: Advances in Knowledge Organization, vol. 12. Ergon Verlag, Würzburg, pp. 91–97.

López-Huertas, M.J., Barité, M., de Torres, I., 2004. Terminological representation of specialized areas in conceptual structures: the case of gender studies. In: McIlwaine, I.C. (Ed.), Knowledge Organization and the Global Information Society; Proceedings of the Eighth International ISKO Conference, 13–16 July, London, UK. In: Advances in Knowledge Organization, vol. 9. Ergon Verlag, Würzburg, pp. 35–39.

Madalli, D.P., Preedip Balaji, B., Sarangi, A.K., 2014. Music domain analysis for building faceted ontological representation. In: Babik, W. (Ed.), Knowledge organization in the 21st century: Between Historical Patterns and Future Prospects, Proceedings of the 13th International ISKO Conference, Krakow, Poland, 19–22 May 2014. In: Advances in Knowledge Organization, vol. 14. Ergon-Verlag, Würzburg, pp. 289–296.

Mai, J.-E., 1999. A post-modern theory of knowledge organization. In: Woods, L. (Ed.), Proceedings of the 62nd Annual Meeting of the American Society for Information Science Information Today, Medford, NJ, pp. 547–556.

Manzi, S., 2009. Classifying philosophy at the library of the Scuola Normale Superiore (Pi Italy): part B: evaluation and experience. Knowl. Organ. 36, 146–149.

Marchese, C., Smiraglia, R.P., 2013. Boundary objects: CWA, an HR firm, and eme′ vocabulary. Knowl. Organ. 40, 254–259.

Meireles, M.R.G., Cendón, B.V., de Almeida, P.E.M., 2014. Bibliometric knowledge ′ zation: a domain analytic method using artificial neural networks. Knowl. 41, 145–159.

Ménard, E., Dorey, J., 2014. TIIARA: a new bilingual taxonomy for image indexir′ Organ. 41, 113–122.

Miguel, S., Moya-Anegón, F., Herrero-Solana, V., 2008. A new approach to domain analysis: multilevel research fronts structure. Scientometrics 74, 3′

Miller, S.J., Fox, M.J., Lee, H.-L., Olson, H.A., 2006. Great expectations: pro′ ception and knowledge organization curricula. In: Budin, G., Swertz, C (Eds.), Knowledge Organization and the Global Learning Society; P′ 9th ISKO International Conference, Vienna, 4–7 July 2006. In: Adva′ Organization, vol. 10. Ergon Verlag, Würzburg, pp. 349–358.

*R*i

Munk, T.B., Mørk, K., 2007. Folksonomies, tagging communities, and tagging strategies: an empirical study. Knowl. Organ. 34, 115–127.

Mustafa El Hadi, W., 2008. Discourse community analysis: sense construction versus non-sense construction. In: Arsenault, C., Tennis, J. (Eds.), Culture and Identity in Knowledge Organization: Proceedings of the 10th International ISKO Conference, Montréal, 5–8 August 2008. In: Advances in Knowledge Organization, vol. 11. Ergon Verlag, Würzburg, pp. 302–306.

Nascimento, D.M., Marteleto, R.M., 2008. Social field, domains of knowledge and informational practice. J. Doc. 64, 397–412.

Neelameghan, A., Raghavan, K.S., 2014. Science of consciousness as a domain: issues for knowledge organization. In: Babik, W. (Ed.), Knowledge Organization in the 21st Century: Between Historical Patterns and Future Prospects; Proceedings of the 13th International ISKO Conference, Krakow, Poland, 19–22 May 2014. In: Advances in Knowledge Organization, vol. 14. Ergon-Verlag, Würzburg, pp. 50–56.

Oikarinen, T., Kortelainen, T., 2013. Challenges of diversity, consistency, and globality in indexing of local archeological artifacts. Knowl. Organ. 40, 123–135.

Ørom, A., 2003. Knowledge organization in the domain of art studies—history, transition and conceptual changes. Knowl. Organ. 30, 128–143.

Orrico, E., Dodebei, V., Gontijo, M., 2012. The precision of metaphor for information retrieval. In: Neelameghan, A., Raghavan, K.S. (Eds.), Categories, Contexts, and Relations in Knowledge Organization: Proceedings of the Twelfth International ISKO Conference, 6–9 August 2012, Mysore, India. In: Advances in Knowledge Organization, vol. 13. Ergon Verlag, Würzburg, pp. 103–108.

Ou, S., Khoo, C., Goh, D.H., Heng, H.-Y., 2004. Automatic discourse parsing of sociology dissertation abstracts as sentence categorization. In: McIlwaine, I.C. (Ed.), Knowledge Organization and the Global Information Society; Proceedings of the Eighth International ISKO Conference, 13–16 July, London, UK. In: Advances in Knowledge Organization, vol. 9. Ergon Verlag, Würzburg, pp. 345–350.

Pajarillo, E.J.Y., 2006. A qualitative research on the use of knowledge organization in nursing information behavior. In: Budin, G., Swertz, C., Mitgutsch, K. (Eds.), Knowledge Organization and the Global Learning Society; Proceedings of the 9th ISKO International Conference, Vienna, 4–7 July 2006. In: Advances in Knowledge Organization, vol. 10. Ergon Verlag, Würzbur, pp. 311–322.

Pattuelli, C., Rubinow, S., 2013. The knowledge organization of DBpedia: a case study. J. Doc. 69 (6), 762–772.

Pinto, V.B., Rabelo, C.R. de O., Girão, I.P.T., 2014. SNOMED-CT as standard language for organization and representation of the information in patient records. Knowl. Organ. 41, 311–318.

Rafferty, P., 2010. Genre theory, knowledge organisation and fiction. In: Gnoli, C., Mazzochi, F. (Eds.), Paradigms and Conceptual Systems in Knowledge Organization, Proceedings of the 11th International ISKO Conference, 23–26 February 2010, Rome, Italy. In: Advances in Knowledge Organization, vol. 12. Ergon Verlag, Würzburg, pp. 254–261.

Raghavan, K.S., Ravichandra Rao, I.K., 2014. Facets of facet analysis: a domain analysis. In: Babik, W. (Ed.), Knowledge Organization in the 21st Century: Between Historical Patterns and Future Prospects, Proceedings of the 13th International ISKO Conference, Krakow, Poland, 19–22 May 2014. In: Advances in Knowledge Organization, vol. 14. Ergon-Verlag, Würzburg, pp. 107–113.

Ribeiro, F., 2014. The use of classification in archives as a means of organization, representation and retrieval of information. Knowl. Organ. 41, 319–326.

Sanatjoo, A., 2010. Development of thesaurus structure through a work-task oriented methodology. In: Gnoli, C., Mazzochi, F. (Eds.), Paradigms and Conceptual Systems in Knowledge Organization, Proceedings of the 11th International ISKO Conference, 23–26 February 2010, Rome, Italy. In: Advances in Knowledge Organization, vol. 12. Ergon Verlag, Würzburg, pp. 216–222.

Scaturro, I., 2013. Faceted taxonomies for the performing arts domain: the case of the European collected library of artistic performance. Knowl. Organ. 40, 205–211.

Smiraglia, R.P., 2006. Music information retrieval: an example of Bates' substrate? In: Moukdad, H. (Ed.), Information Science Revisited: Approaches to Innovation: Proceedings of the Canadian Association for Information Science Annual Conference, 1–3 June 2006. Available http://www.cais-acsi.ca/search.asp?year=2006.

Smiraglia, R.P., 2007. Two kinds of power: insight into the legacy of Patrick Wilson. In: Dalkir, K., Arsenault, C. (Eds.), Information Sharing in a Fragmented World: Crossing Boundaries: Proceedings of the Canadian Association for Information Science Annual Conference, 12–15 May 2007. Available http://www.caisacsi.ca/2007proceedings.htm.

Smiraglia, R., 2009a. Redefining the "s" in ISMIR: visualizing the evolution of a domain. In: Rothbauer, P., Stevenson, S., Wathen, N. (Eds.), Mapping the 21st Century Information Landscape: Borders, Bridges and Byways: Proceedings of the 37th Annual CAIS/ACSI Conference, 28–30 May 2009, Ottawa, Ontario, Canada. Available http://www.cais-acsi.ca/search.asp?year=2009.

Smiraglia, R.P., 2009b. Modulation and specialization in North American knowledge organization: visualizing pioneers. In: Jacob, E.K., Barbara, K. (Eds.), Proceedings of the 2nd North American Symposium on Knowledge Organization, June 17–18, 2009. Available http://hdl.handle.net/10150/105092.

Smiraglia, R.P., 2011. Domain coherence within knowledge organization: people, interacting theoretically, across geopolitical and cultural boundaries. In: McKenzie, P., Johnson, C., Stevenson, S. (Eds.), Exploring Interactions of People, Places and Information, Proceedings of the 39th Annual CAIS/ACSI Conference, University of New Brunswick, Fredericton, N. B. Canada, 2–4 June 2011. Available http://www.cais-acsi.ca/conferences.htm.

Smiraglia, R.P., 2012. Universes, dimensions, domains, intensions and extensions: knowledge organization for the 21st century. In: Neelameghan, A., Raghavan, K.S. (Eds.), Categories, Contexts, and Relations in Knowledge Organization: Proceedings of the Twelfth International ISKO Conference, 6–9 August 2012, Mysore, India. In: Advances in Knowledge Organization, vol. 13. Ergon Verlag, Würzburg, pp. 1–7.

Smiraglia, R.P., 2013a. The epistemological dimension of knowledge organization. IRIS: Informação, Memória e Tecnologia 2 (1), 2–11.

Smiraglia, R.P., 2013b. Is FRBR a domain? Domain analysis applied to the literature of *The FRBR Family of Conceptual Models*. Knowl. Organ. 40, 273–282.

Smiraglia, R.P., 2013c. Prolegomena to a new order: a domain-analytical review of the influence of S.R. Ranganathan on knowledge organization. SRELS J. Inform. Manag. 50 (6), 709–719.

Souza, R.R., Tudhope, D., Almeida, M.B., 2012. Towards a taxonomy of KOS: dimensions for classifying knowledge organization systems. Knowl. Organ. 39, 179–192.

Sundin, O., 2003. Towards an understanding of symbolic aspects of professional information: an analysis of the nursing knowledge domain. Knowl. Organ. 30, 170–181.

Tanaka, M., 2010. Domain analysis of computational science: fifty years of a scientific computing group. In: Gnoli, C., Mazzochi, F. (Eds.), Paradigms and Conceptual Systems in Knowledge Organization, Proceedings of the 11th International ISKO Conference, 23–26 February 2010, Rome, Italy. In: Advances in Knowledge Organization, vol. 12. Ergon Verlag, Würzburg, pp. 248–253.

Tian, L., Zhiping, Y., Zhengyin, H., 2013. The large aperture optical elements patent search system based on domain knowledge. World Patent Inf. 35 (3), 209–213. http://dx.doi.org/10.1016/j.wpi.2013.04.007, Sept. 2013. 5p.

Vinod Kumar, B.L., Nikam, K., 2014. Development of an information support system for yogic science using knowledge organization systems. Knowl. Organ. 41, 288–295.

Weller, K., 2014. What do we get from Twitter—and what not? A close look at Twitter research in the social sciences. Knowl. Organ. 41, 238–248.

Youlin, Z., Nunes, J.M.B., Zhonghua, D., 2014. Construction and evolution of a Chinese Information Science and Information Service (CIS&IS) onto-thesaurus. Knowl. Organ. 41, 131–144.

Zemmels, D., 2014. Accessing virtual social worlds: a unique methodology for research in new media spaces. Knowl. Organ. 41, 230–237.

Zhao, R., Wu, S., 2014. The network pattern of journal knowledge transfer in library and information science in China. Knowl. Organ. 41, 276–287.

Zherebchevsky, S., 2010. Formalism in knowledge organization: thematic analysis of ISKO 10 proceedings. In: Gnoli, C., Mazzochi, F. (Eds.), Paradigms and Conceptual Systems in Knowledge Organization, Proceedings of the 11th International ISKO Conference, 23–26 February 2010, Rome, Italy. In: Advances in Knowledge Organization, vol. 12. Ergon Verlag, Würzburg, pp. 98–105.

Zins, C., Guttman, D., 2003. Domain analysis of social work: an example of an integrated methodological approach. Knowl. Organ. 30, 196–212.

Empirical methods for visualizing domains

3

3.1 Capturing a knowledge base

At the simplest level, domain analysis simply means capturing the knowledge base of a community. Obviously, there are many ways to go about such a thing, and the choice of methods depends entirely on the specific context. That is, the demands of the KOS to be developed will dictate all of the aspects of methodology applicable in any given case. For example, one could posit knowledge organization as a domain and set about creating a KOS for knowledge organization. In both cases—the domain and the application—these terms are much too broad to be useful for research or development. One must consider whether to create an ontology, thesaurus, classification, or some other sort of KOS and at what level of specificity. At the same time, there are many possible ways to define a domain within the larger concept of knowledge organization—one could work with ISKO proceedings, or ISKO conference programs, or participants attending an ISKO conference; one could choose *Knowledge Organization* the journal, or graduate (or undergraduate) iSchool knowledge organization curricula, or any definitive monograph (such as Svenonius' (2001) *The Intellectual Foundation of Information Organization* or Smiraglia's (2014) *The Elements of Knowledge Organization*), or some combination of these. The specific context will dictate the intension and extension of the domain. The extension will be populated by the metalevel terms or classes of concepts, and the intension will be populated by discoverable granular concepts or terms. But the nature of the eventual KOS developed will be determined by the culture and context as well. The intension and extension of data from a real-time Delphi study of conference participants will be different from those derived from the program of their conference, or their papers published in the proceedings, or discourse resulting from interacting texts, and so on.

With that caveat as a starting point, this chapter is devoted to explication of the typical or standard approaches to capturing the knowledge base of a community, in other words, domain analysis for knowledge organization. In every case, the methods employed are considered to be empirical because in every case the results arise from actual knowledge use within the community. The word empirical means arising from direct experience, and methodologically is used to mean results derived from observation or experience, in particular, controlled observation or experience. It means that because we want to know exactly what the knowledge base is of our target community, we will attempt to capture that knowledge base directly from the community either by observing it at work, or by experiencing its function. Terms can be extracted easily from textual resources, yielding an empirical (observed) list of terms bounded by the particular resource. Concepts can be captured by ethnological means by participating in the activity of the community and experiencing directly the conceptual base in use at a particular moment or over several moments in time. In either case, because the methods involve direct observation or experience, we may say that our results are empirical. Empirical results often are contrasted with results compiled by rational means, which is to say, generated by indirect thought experiment rather than direct experience. In the current knowledge organization paradigm, empirical results are considered critical for generating domain-specific knowledge bases for KOS.

How we go about capturing this knowledge base, specifically, is what constitutes our domain-analytical methodology. A methodology is a plan for research that quite specifically lays out which tools will be used and why. Research methods are sometimes seen as endemic to specific domains, but in reality, they are simply tightly controlled models for information discovery. By tightly controlled I mean that research methods are designed either to rule out bias altogether or to acknowledge and embrace it. Experiments are conducted with control groups, to whom no treatment is administered, so as to have comparable data about the effect of the treatment. Time-series analyses are conducted against a backdrop of real-world events, to rule out biases from outside the lab, and are controlled to rule out "historical" biases, which are those learned by the participants during the course of the experiment. But ethnographic studies require total involvement in the community so as better to understand the interactions taking place. Research methods, in general, are the subject of many textbooks, all of which are potentially relevant in domain analysis. In this book, my focus is specifically on techniques for capturing the knowledge base of a community.

The final keyword for this chapter is visualizing. What does it mean to visualize a domain? It means to find a way to make the abstract momentarily concrete. Visualization also means synergistically to expand perception by adding understanding beyond that of the textual narrative or data. Charts and diagrams are typical means of visualizing research results. Here is a visualization I created for a research paper on social tagging, in which I wanted to make the point that perception (*eidetic description*, from phenomenology, refers to motion from observation to perception) is a process of multiple syntheses springing from observation (Figure 3.1).

The surrounding text explains the concept in some detail, but the visualization helps expand understanding by reinforcing the concept of visual input followed by multiple syntheses. In domain analysis, we have several common techniques for visualizing the knowledge base of domains. Other techniques are applicable, and new techniques are as frequent as a new software. We will survey the most common here and discuss how new visualizations might improve the "picture" of a domain.

3.2   Taxonomy of domain-analytical approaches

We already have visited Hjørland's (2002) 11 approaches to domain analysis several times. In the conclusion of Chapter 2, we agreed to alter the list slightly. Here is the current list, which we now see is a sort of taxonomy, still with 11 elements:

Subject pathfinders
Special classifications and thesauri

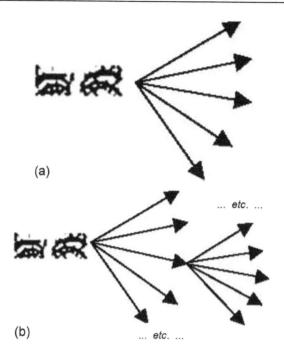

Figure 3.1 Visualization of phenomenological synthesis: (a) Eidetic description and (b) eidetic description is synthesis (Smiraglia, 2008, p. 255).

Empirical user studies
Informetric studies
Historical studies
Document and genre studies
Epistemological and critical studies
Terminological studies
Database semantics
Discourse analyses
Cognition, expert knowledge, and AI

To some extent, all of these are empirical, because all of them are based on observing the experiences of specialists working in their own domains. Rather than reiterate Hjørland's text again, I will use this space to discuss some of the analytical parameters that are implicit in the taxonomy. Rather like a photographer hopping about photographing a still life from different points of view, angles, perspectives, and trajectories, the domain analyst is encouraged to consider the activity of the domain in question, and to do so exhaustively. We begin by considering the work of the community, what they do, how they do it, what they produce, and all of the variations of each that can be considered. We are concerned with the context in which the community operates. We must identify the specific actors and the roles they play in the community. We must identify the goals, objectives, and methods used by the community. And we must discover the underlying knowledge base, in the form of an ontology, which is the shared province of the specific community. In this sense, we are encouraging a case-study-like focus on every aspect of the group (discourse community, domain, workplace, etc.) that can be captured.

3.3   An example: A pharmacy

We may begin with a fairly simple generic example of a pharmacy. A pharmacy dispenses medications. In order to dispense medications, it is necessary for it to have on hand, or be able quickly to acquire, necessary medications. This means that the community of actors (employees) must know and track their clients (also actors) accurately so as to plan to acquire and dispense medications as needed, without wasting undispensed medication, and without causing client problems if a specific medication is not available. At this point in this example I have introduced one product, two actors, and two trajectories, and by implication, the connections among them: medications (which I have not defined further), pharmacy employees and clients, processes of acquisition and dispensation, and client-based knowledge gathering and management. Each of these aspects must further be understood completely. Let us use a simple image to visualize these domain components (Figure 3.2).

The actors described so far as pharmacy employees actually comprise a group with several different kinds of actors, pharmacists, pharmacy assistants, and cashiers in all likelihood. In some parts of the United States, pharmacies are beginning also to provide licensed practical nurses and physician's assistants to conduct patient examinations on-site. Each group of actors potentially has its own knowledge base, its own vocabulary, and its own set(s) of procedures. To the extent that the actor groups share vocabulary the domain has one coherent ontology, but to the extent that they have vocabularies peculiar to their activity bases, the possibility exists that the domain comprises several overlapping ontologies. In either event, the points of overlap constitute boundary objects, which are a kind of pivot point (Marchese and Smiraglia, 2013) allowing the groups to speak with each other. Even where a single ontology can be asserted, chances are good that different epistemological points of view inhere in

Figure 3.2 Actors, products, processes in a pharmacy.

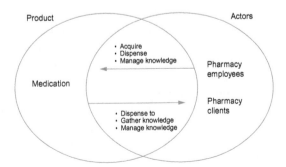

the different sets of actor procedures, as well as in the different backgrounds of actor education, training, and experience. The client actors, of course, comprise all sorts of diverse cultural and demographic characteristics, all of which influence their own ontologies. In this case, we want to isolate the client vocabulary to just that which is employed in this domain, when they interact with the pharmacy. The acquisition of medications is quite a different set of activities from their dispensation, requiring overlapping but distinct work-based ontologies as well. The medications, of course, also are complex, some by prescription (requiring interaction with a third group of external actors, the medical providers for the clients), and some are over-the-counter products. The domain analyst's tasks involve empirical capture of ontologies, epistemologies, controlled vocabularies, classifications, as well as textual material accompanying both the medications and the procedures. The domain analyst further must engage in empirical capture of the work and interaction of the actor groups. Let us now reconsider this analysis in terms of our taxonomy of approaches to domain analysis.

Subject pathfinders were useful tools created by librarians in the last decades of the twentieth century, often in the form of pamphlets that could be passed out at the reference desk. In the first decades of the twenty-first century, these have become Web-based instructional guides for finding informational literature in precise categories. We could easily see how the plethora of printed drug data that accompanies distributed pharmaceuticals falls into this category. I often am appalled at the amount of paper handed to me when I go to pick up a bottle of pills; all of what they hand to me is available on the Web, in a variety of downloadable formats, under the keyword of the name of the specific drug, or even its generic equivalent. These are literature guides when they narrate the medication and point to the research literature, and they are subject gateways when we search them on the Web and find links to user experiences, prescribing guidelines, and so forth. Here (Figure 3.2) is a Google screen capture for Azithromycin, a common antibiotic.

If you look closely at this illustration, you will learn that I searched for this under its nickname "Z-pack" which is what doctors call it when they tell me they are prescribing it. The nickname comes from the fact that the medication comes in a box of precise doses to be taken one per day over a 5-day period—thus, a "pack." You also will see that the official pharmaceutical definition appears in a dictionary-like box on the right, with basic terms, definitions, and links. On the left are links to Websites where one can read about the experimental research that authorized the medication, or user experiences of side effects, or practical advice about how to cope with side effects, and explanations about the different ways of prescribing the medication. For our purposes it is interesting to note the quantity of data just in response to one query about one pharmaceutical. On the other hand, if we were to analyze the text on this page for word frequency, we would learn quite a lot about the domains or contexts in which this antibiotic figures (Figure 3.3).

This word cloud represents 395 words appearing on the Google search page shown in Figure 3.2, of which 203 are unique (roughly 20 words appear in each result line). The most frequently used terms are Azithromycin, Zythromax, Z-pak, and Z-pack. This visualization comes from Voyant, a visualization tool created by Sinclair and Rockwell (2009). It shows us also the contextual data: antibiotic and infectious,

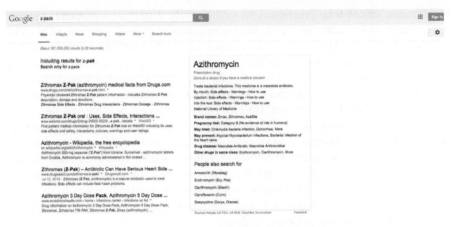

Figure 3.3 Screen shot of Google search result for "Z-pack."

Figure 3.4 Word cloud visualizing word frequency in Figure 3.2, created using Voyant (http://voyant-tools.org/).

medical interactions and information, and so on. The frequency distribution itself tells us which words are most prevalent and which are not. The visualization expands understanding both with size and prominence but also by surrounding the most frequently used words with contextual granular terms. Please note, this is empirical domain analysis, using one term, from one variable, in one domain context.

To continue, we might consider that there are already specialized classifications and thesauri for pharmaceuticals, including their generic and commercial names, and for maladies and prescribing practices. These range from the National Library of Medicine's *Medical Subject Headings* (*MeSH*) to NLM's taxonomy database (http://www.ncbi.nlm.nih.gov/taxonomy), and many more. The Wikipedia entry for Azithromycin lists 11 coded identifiers, indicating at least that many classifications exist containing this pharmaceutical. Other medical and scientific classifications (e.g., such as insurance codes) will be part of the interactions in our simple pharmacy example. In addition, we might wish to capture the ontologies (or knowledge bases) of the sets of actors in the pharmacy. We might do this through ethnographic means, in particular through participant observation such as that employed in cognitive work analysis (CWA). We will discuss CWA in greater detail in Chapter 5, but for now it is enough to understand it as a means for analyzing the work and work ontology of a community. In this case, we would be examining the interacting work and work ontologies of several different sets of actors (e.g., pharmacists, clients, medical personnel) as well as the different task-defined actors or subgroups working in the pharmacy itself. We most likely here would uncover what are called boundary objects, or terms that are used as points of communication between diverse actor groups. We might also expect to observe epistemological differences among the groups, particularly between the clients and the pharmacists. We did not posit an information system in our example, although one is implicit in the communicating functions of the various actors. We might employ user studies to analyze the efficacy of vocabularies and search mechanisms encountered directly by clients.

This example is deliberately vague or generic, in order to simplify it as an illustrative tool. Had we added cultural factors (such as geographic location or language) the example would have become much more complex. This is because domains are complex and are in complex relationships with other domains. In this simple example we encountered several taxonomic approaches, including pathfinders, special classifications, indexing specialties, empirical user studies, epistemological studies, and terminological studies. It would not be too much of a stretch to then expand our study with informetric and historical studies of the literatures produced adjacent to this simple work environment. In every case, domain analysis helps us capture, extract, and synthesize the knowledge base(s) of the community at hand, and visualization of results helps us to expand understanding and perception of those knowledge bases.

But it is important methodologically to understand that a single research project is never enough to fully embrace and analyze any domain or to extract more than a temporal moment in its knowledge base. It takes many studies, of different sorts and at different times, not only to generate a full description of the domain but also to comprehend its evolution and the manner in which an individual research result fits into a larger visualization of knowledge organization. In the end, each domain-analytical study is simply one more step, presumably the next appropriate step on a research trajectory.

3.4 Domain analysis is contextually driven

What we can learn from our pharmacy example is that domain analysis always is con-
textually driven. That is, it always takes place in not just a single isolated context but
also in the vicinity of neighboring, overlapping, parallel, and even tandem contexts.
We can easily isolate the knowledge base of the workers in our pharmacy and generate
a KOS based on it. But we must acknowledge the neighboring domains, such as pharmaceuticals, medicine, and healthcare, and the domains that neighbor them as well,
such as chemistry, biology, nursing, social work, and so forth. The context of even
a single domain-analytical study is critical for the isolation and evolution of the
knowledge base extracted. But for the theoretical value of the analysis of a single
domain, we must look to its contribution alongside its contextual neighbors as well.
We will return to this notion in the final chapter of the book. For now it is simply
important to remember that in any empirical analysis we must define the context precisely and with reference to neighboring contexts.

One final lesson from our analysis is that although we have a large taxonomy of
approaches to domain analysis not only beginning with those proposed by Hjørland
but also incorporating the better defined intensional categories observed in
Chapter 2, the "approaches" do not exactly coincide with specific methods. That
is, we have a very large set of empirical methods for extracting the knowledge bases
of discourse communities, any or all of which can be used in combination as appropriate whether employed for the design of a classification, a thesaurus, an ontology, a
pathfinder, a metadata schema, or some other kind of knowledge organization system.
These methods will be the subject of the next two chapters.

Approaches such as historical, epistemological, and genre analyses and analyses
using critical theory are not, strictly speaking, empirical approaches in nature because
they do not rely on straightforward, observable, and replicable techniques for term
extraction and ontology orientation. Rather, these approaches rely on the analysis
of artifacts such as documents for secondary evidence that can be used to understand
the intellectual functioning of domains. We will discuss these methods briefly in the
beginning of the final chapter below.

3.5 Operationalizing domains for analysis

Let us return briefly, then, to our definition of a domain (Smiraglia, 2012, p. 114):

*A domain is best understood as a unit of analysis for the construction of a KOS. That
is, a domain is a group with an ontological base that reveals an underlying teleology,
a set of common hypotheses, epistemological consensus on methodological
approaches, and social semantics. If, after the conduct of systematic analysis, no consensus on these points emerges, then neither intension nor extension can be defined,
and the group thus does not constitute a domain.*

By unpacking its elements, we can find operational parameters for domain-analytic research. The context is set by the opening sentence; the domain we are seeking to analyze is in the first instance a unit of analysis for the construction of a knowledge organization system. Whether it is our intent immediately to construct such a system or to leave it for others in subsequent work, our purpose in unraveling the extension and intension of a domain is to ascertain the concepts and their characteristics that constitute the functional knowledge base of the community under consideration.

The second consideration is that a domain is a group. As we have seen in our review of knowledge organization domain-analytical research in Chapter 2, it is possible to define almost any conceptual cluster as a domain, so long as it has produced a record sufficient for analysis. It would even be possible to analyze a group that had produced no tangible intellectual records by use of ethnographic means. Methodologically then, the unit of analysis must be, in some way, a visible functional group. Some aspects of domain analysis, such as the simple demographic measures described in Chapter 4 will have as their focus an attempt to demonstrate the group's coherence in terms of its membership and longevity.

Then, once these conditions are satisfied—that is, we are certain we have a definable and functional group and can visualize its need for and use of a knowledge organization system—the remaining aspects of a domain that can be extracted by analysis are these:

- An ontological base that reveals an underlying teleology—does the group share a common goal that is implicit or explicit in its knowledge base?
- A set of common hypotheses—is there a theoretical paradigm in operation? If so, it will dictate the hypotheses used in the domain for testing theoretical parameters. In nonscholarly domains, we can consider a parallel consideration to apply to means employed by the group to contribute to the evolution of its common goal.
- An epistemological consensus on methodological approaches—most domains that embrace a single theoretical paradigm (or a consistent set of such paradigms) will share methodological approaches rooted in different epistemological points of view.
- Social semantics—at the simplest level this simply means that the group should be visibly in conversation utilizing its common ontology. At higher levels of complexity it means that there should be records of communication and exchange of ideas; in scholarly domains citation, intercitation, and cocitation will be evidence of social semantics.

Any or all of the empirical methods described in Chapter 4, such as term extraction, thematic analysis, and visualization of author cocitation clusters should point to these aspects of domain coherence. The search for any one in a defined domain is sufficient to constitute an individual research project. The research objectives determine the applicable methodology. A search for a common ontology suggests some form of term extraction. An analysis of epistemic influences suggests some form of discourse analysis. Any or all of these methods may be combined to provide methodological triangulation for a richer picture of a coherent domain.

References

Hjørland, B., 2002. Domain analysis in information science: eleven approaches—traditional as well as innovative. J. Doc. 58, 422–462.

Marchese, C., Smiraglia, R.P., 2013. Boundary objects: CWA, an HR firm, and emergent vocabulary. Knowl. Organ. 40, 254–259.

Sinclair, S., Rockwell, G., 2009. Hermeneuti.ca: the rhetoric of text analysis. Available: http://hermeneuti.ca/.

Smiraglia, R.P., 2008. Noesis: perception and every day classification. In: Arsenault, C., Tennis, J. (Eds.), Culture and Identity in Knowledge Organization: Proceedings of the 10th International ISKO Conference, Montréal, 5–8 August 2008. In: Advances in Knowledge Organization, vol. 11. Ergon Verlag, Würzburg, pp. 249–253.

Smiraglia, R.P., 2012. Epistemology of domain analysis. In: Smiraglia, R.P., Lee, H. (Eds.), Cultural Frames of Knowledge. Ergon, Würzburg, pp. 111–124.

Smiraglia, R.P., 2014. The Elements of Knowledge Organization. Springer, New York.

Svenonius, E., 2001. The Intellectual Foundation of Information Organization. MIT Press, Cambridge.

Empirical techniques for visualizing domains

4

4.1 Introduction to empirical techniques

As we have seen, domain analysis in knowledge organization involves extracting knowledge bases from functioning discourse communities. Many studies of domain analysis use a mixture of evidentiary approaches to extract or generate terminology and its ontological context. Empirical techniques will be explained in this chapter, with a focus on demonstrating domain coherence—by demarcating group membership, focus, and function—and then on actual extraction of ontological content using citation analysis, coword analysis, author cocitation analysis, and network analysis. The techniques are in wide use in information science (IS), so the focus here will be on their use for domain analysis in knowledge organization and on means of visualizing domain coherence. An interesting point to make early on is that, despite the quantitative origins of the analytical methods employed in domain analysis, a qualitative aspect is present as well in the appropriate definition of the domain under analysis. Decisions about sources, about taxonomic depth, about cluster definition, and interpretation of results are all dependent to some extent on the researcher's detailed comprehension of the domain.

4.2 Evidentiary sources for citation analysis: *Web of Science* and *Scopus*

The most common metrical methods employed in domain analysis are those based on various forms of citation analysis. Citations represent social semantics in a discourse community. That is, scholars indicate shared meaning by stating their reliance on each other's writings. So we can see citations as a kind of trace evidence of associations among members of a discourse community; an assumption of citation analysis is that meaning (or topicality) are at the root of citing relationships. Authors in a citing relationship also might be connected to the same theoretical paradigm. Citations are a ready source of evidence in published documents, and basic citation analyses can give good indications about the parameters of a domain.

One problem for domain analysis is that there is a lack of commercial indexing for new and evolving domains, or for domains that have not achieved a certain critical mass of influence among scholarly disciplines. The most useful commercial indexing services for domain analysis are the Thomson Reuters' *Web of Science* and Elsevier's *Scopus*. If the domain under scrutiny is included in either corpus, a number of simple indicative measures can be generated almost instantly. All of them can be used to define parameters of domains for knowledge organization. Frequently these quantitative data can be used together with other more qualitative results to interpret and visualize the extension and intension of domains.

4.2.1   Web of Science *as a source*

Web of Science™ is the successor to decades of citation analysis and indexing stemming from the legendary Eugene Garfield's Institute for Scientific Information. Now owned by large global publishing conglomerate Thomson Reuters and incorporated into the research platform Web of Knowledge™, the *Web of Science*™ represents an immense accumulation of not only indexed references, but also citations, intercitations, journal productivity, impact factors, and so forth. The core *Web of Science*™ collection includes the *Science Citation Index, Social Sciences Citation Index*, and *Arts & Humanities Citation Index. Journal Citation Reports (JCR)* is also included. Only domains adjudged sufficiently influential by the managers of the corpus are included, which means that rather many domains that might be the subject of KO research are not indexed. In fact, only some aspects of knowledge organization (the journal *Knowledge Organization*, but not biennial international proceedings) are indexed. It is also problematic that many institutions do not subscribe to the entire indexed corpus. The illustrations here are produced from a subscription that indexes works from 1987 to the present. Many tutorials and online training modules are available from Thomson Reuters; the material below is intended to illustrate how to begin using *Web of Science*™ (*WoS*) for knowledge organization domain analysis.

To begin, domains can be defined in sufficient detail to yield informative data fairly easily. To follow-on from our pharmacy example in Chapter 3, a "basic search" for the term "pharmacy" yields more than 22,000 results. Here is an instance where many potentially different choices could be made concerning the definition of domain parameters, all of which will affect the outcome of the analysis. In every case it is critical to document the decision making, not only to explain the outcome but also to permit future replication. In this case, a number of options for refining a search are presented, including a list of "Web of Science Categories" that shows how many cited works are in each category. A screen with the first 100 options offers several smaller, related domains. "Computer science information systems" has 109 cited works, so I have chosen that for this example. The search thus refined yields the opening results page shown in Figure 4.1.

To begin we can see that each cited work has a complete reference, with links to an abstract or to full text (where your institution subscribes to the journals involved). Also, we see the search terms highlighted in titles of the cited works. These have been sorted by publication date, most recent first. We can adjust the sort order to sort by author, relevance, title, conference, currency, or citation rate; Figure 4.2 shows the first screen of the result sorted by citation rate in descending order.

We can see already some basic results. There are 97 articles and 18 proceeding papers in the result. Most populous research areas and most productive authors in the result can easily be displayed (Figure 4.3). "Analyze Results" takes us to a menu where we may request various analyses of the 109 citation result. Figure 4.4 shows the top 10 authors.

Figure 4.1 *WoS* subject search "Pharmacy—Computer science information systems."

Figure 4.2 *WoS* subject search "Pharmacy—Computer science information systems" in descending citation order.

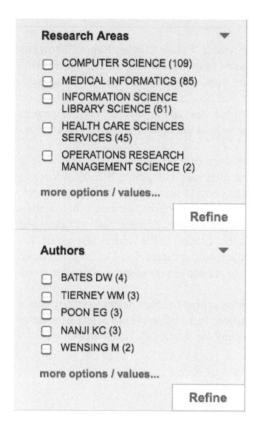

Figure 4.3 *WoS* search: research areas, productive authors.

WEB OF SCIENCE™   THOMSON REUTERS™

Results Analysis

<<Back to previous page

109 records. TOPIC: (pharmacy)
Analysis: WEB OF SCIENCE CATEGORIES: (COMPUTER SCIENCE INFORMATION SYSTEMS)

Rank the records by this field:	Set display options:	Sort by:
Organisations-Enhanced / Publication Years / Research Areas / Source Titles / Web of Science Categories ▾	Show the top 10 ▾ Results. Minimum record count (threshold): 2	⊙Record count ○Selected field

Analyze

Use the checkboxes below to view the records. You can choose to view those selected records, or you can exclude them (and view the others).

☐ View Records / ✕ Exclude Records	Field: Authors	Record Count	% of 109	Bar Chart	Save Analysis Data to File ⊙Data rows displayed in table ○All data rows (up to 200,000)
☐	BATES DW	4	3.670 %	ı	
☐	TIERNEY WM	3	2.752 %	ı	
☐	POON EG	3	2.752 %	ı	
☐	NANJI KC	3	2.752 %	ı	
☐	WINSLADE N	2	1.835 %	ı	
☐	WENSING M	2	1.835 %	ı	
☐	VAN DER SIJS H	2	1.835 %	ı	
☐	VAN DEN BEMT PMLA	2	1.835 %	ı	
☐	TSUI FC	2	1.835 %	ı	
☐	THOMAS CP	2	1.835 %	ı	

☐ View Records / ✕ Exclude Records	Field: Authors	Record Count	% of 109	Bar Chart	Save Analysis Data to File ○Data rows displayed in table ○All data rows (up to 200,000)

(33 Authors value(s) outside display options.)

Figure 4.4 *WoS* search top 10 authors.

Figure 4.5 shows the top 10 publication years. "Create Citation Report" shows us some metrics about citations and publications in the result over time (Figure 4.6).

We can see that these 109 words were cited 1644 times, mostly without self-citations by 1514 citing articles. We can link to the citing articles by clicking on the number in that result (to the right of the bar chart at the top). We see the average number of citations per item is 15.08. And we can see easily the number of citations per year per work.

Figure 4.7 shows the display for one document in our result; in this case a bibliometric analysis of pharmacology and pharmacy comparing *Web of Science* to *Scopus*. We can see that this article has been cited 14 times, that it has 23 references, most of its citations are in the *Web of Science* core collection, but there is one citation in the BIOSIS citation index, one citation in the Chinese Science citation index, and two in SciELO citation index. The most recent citation to the work is also given. We can click on "View Citation Map" to see the result in Figure 4.8. The colors indicate the citation action is from bottom to top; and we can see both works citing this work, and works cited by this work.

We also can search for a specific author by setting the parameters to author search and entering the name of our author "Gorraiz, Juan." The system offers us a set of domains from which to choose, and selecting "technology" yields a display of 29

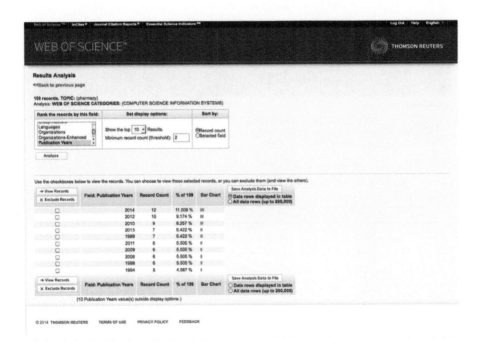

Figure 4.5 *WoS* search top 10 publication years.

Figure 4.6 *WoS* citation report.

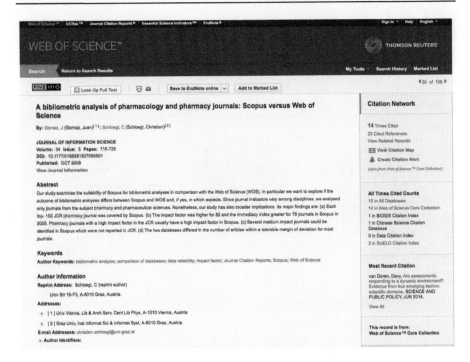

Figure 4.7 *WoS* article by Gorriaz and Schloegel in search result.

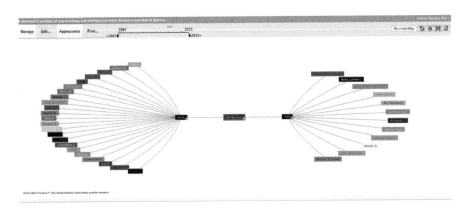

Figure 4.8 *WoS* search citation map.

articles (Figure 4.9). We can create a citation report for this author as well (Figure 4.10).

A cited reference search for "Gorraiz, J*" yields the results in Figure 4.11. I have included only the top of the distribution here. We can click on "view record" (at the right) to see the citing work, and works that cite it, and so on.

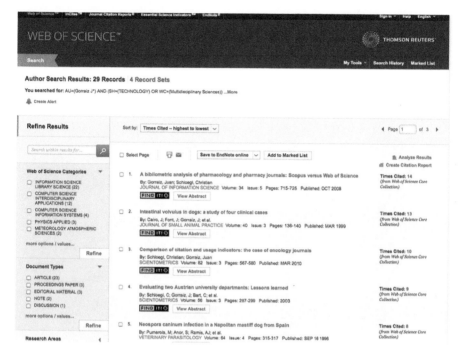

Figure 4.9 *WoS* search for author "Gorraiz, Juan."

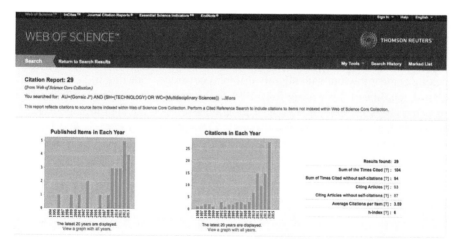

Figure 4.10 *WoS* citation report for author Gorraiz.

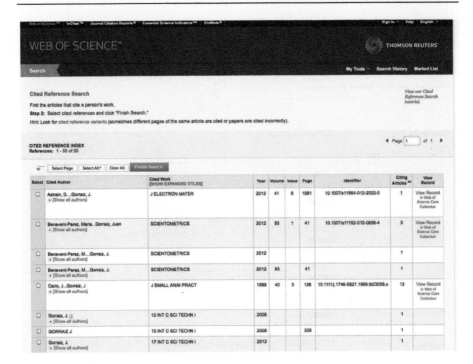

Figure 4.11 *WoS* citation reference search for author Gorraiz.

JCR yields metrics about specific journals. Here, I reproduce screen captures concerning the journal *Knowledge Organization*. Figure 4.12 shows the *JCR* report for the journal. We see a wealth of data, including the impact factor, immediacy index, and cited and citing half-life. Scrolling down shows figures used to calculate these metrics and graphs visualizing some of them. We also can click links for cited and citing journals (Figures 4.13 and 4.14). Finally, Figure 4.15 shows a list of "related journals" developed by *JCR* based on cited and citing relationships.

Scopus is the relatively recently developed citation indexing service from Elsevier, indexing comparably but with slightly different coverage. Indexing in *Scopus* seems to date at the time of this writing from 1995 to the present. Journal coverage is much greater than *WoS* and many more sets of conference proceedings are formally indexed. This means that result sets drawn from both *WoS* and *Scopus* will differ, which leads at least for now to the conclusion that a useful approach to domain analysis is to search both if possible.

4.2.2 Scopus as a source

We can derive comparable, if different from the *WoS*, domain data from *Scopus*. We can begin with the same search for a pharmacy domain. We begin with a "document search" for the term "pharmacy," which yields more than 95,426 results. A list of

ISI Web of Knowledge℠

Journal Citation Reports®

[WELCOME] [HELP] [RETURN TO LIST]

2013 JCR Social Science Edition

Journal: KNOWLEDGE ORGANIZATION

Mark	Journal Title	ISSN	Total Cites	Impact Factor	5-Year Impact Factor	Immediacy Index	Citable Items	Cited Half-life	Citing Half-life
☐	KNOWL ORGAN	0943-7444	144	0.448	0.485	0.167	30	6.3	>10.0

Cited Journal 📊 Citing Journal 📊 Source Data Journal Self Cites

[CITED JOURNAL DATA] [CITING JOURNAL DATA] [📊 IMPACT FACTOR TREND] [RELATED JOURNALS]

Journal Information ⓘ

Full Journal Title: KNOWLEDGE ORGANIZATION
ISO Abbrev. Title: Knowl. Organ.
JCR Abbrev. Title: KNOWL ORGAN
ISSN: 0943-7444
Issues/Year: 4
Language: MULTI-LANGUAGE
Journal Country/Territory: GERMANY
Publisher: ERGON-VERLAG
Publisher Address: GROMBUHLSTR 7, 97080 WURZBURG, GERMANY
Subject Categories: INFORMATION SCIENCE & LIBRARY SCIENCE [VIEW] [🔍 VIEW JOURNAL SUMMARY LIST] [🔍 VIEW CATEGORY DATA]

Journal Rank in Categories: [📊 JOURNAL RANKING]

Eigenfactor® Metrics
Eigenfactor® Score
0.00029
Article Influence® Score
0.134

Journal Impact Factor ⓘ

Cites in 2013 to items published in: 2012 = 12   Number of items published in: 2012 = 35
                                    2011 = 18   2011 = 32
                                    Sum: 30   Sum: 67
Calculation: Cites to recent items 30 = 0.448
             Number of recent items 67

5-Year Journal Impact Factor ⓘ

Cites in (2013) to items published in: 2012 = 12   Number of items published in: 2012 = 35
                                     2011 = 18   2011 = 32
                                     2010 = 3   2010 = 27
                                     2009 = 8   2009 = 21
                                     2008 = 22   2008 = 15
                                     Sum: 63   Sum: 130
Calculation: Cites to recent items 63 = 0.485
                                     130

5-Year Journal Impact Factor ⓘ

Cites in (2013) to items published in: 2012 = 12   Number of items published in: 2012 = 35
                                     2011 = 18   2011 = 32
                                     2010 = 3   2010 = 27
                                     2009 = 8   2009 = 21
                                     2008 = 22   2008 = 15
                                     Sum: 63   Sum: 130
Calculation: Cites to recent items 63 = 0.485
             Number of recent items 130

Journal Self Cites ⓘ

The tables show the contribution of the journal's self cites to its impact factor. This information is also represented in the cited journal graph.

Total Cites	144	Self Cites	58 (40% of 144)
Cites to Years Used in Impact Factor Calculation	30	Self Cites to Years Used in Impact Factor Calculation	15 (50% of 30)
Impact Factor	0.448	Impact Factor without Self Cites	0.224

Journal Immediacy Index ⓘ

Cites in 2013 to items published in 2013 = 5
Number of items published in 2013   = 30
Calculation: Cites to current items   5 = 0.167
             Number of current items 30

Journal Cited Half-Life ⓘ

The cited half-life for the journal is the median age of its items cited in the current JCR year. Half of the citations to the journal are to items published within the cited half-life.
Cited Half-Life: 6.3 years

Breakdown of the citations to the journal by the cumulative percent of 2013 cites to items published in the following years:

Cited Year	2013	2012	2011	2010	2009	2008	2007	2006	2005	2004	2003-all
# Cites from 2013	5	12	18	3	8	22	12	7	4	12	41
Cumulative %	3.47	11.81	24.31	26.39	31.94	47.22	55.56	60.42	63.19	71.53	100

Cited Half-Life Calculations:
The cited half-life calculation finds the number of publication years from the current JCR year that account for 50% of citations received by the journal. Read help for more information on the calculation.

Cited Journal Graph ⓘ
Click here for Cited Journal data table

This graph shows the distribution by cited year of citations to items published in the journal KNOWL ORGAN.
Citations to the Journal (per cited year)

- The white/grey division indicates the cited half-life (if < 10.0). Half of the journal's cited items were published more recently than the cited half-life.
- The top (gold) portion of each column indicates Journal Self Citations: citations to items in the journal from items in the same journal.
- The bottom (blue) portion of each column indicates Non-Self Citations: citations to items in the journal from items in other journals.
- The two lighter columns indicate citations used to calculate the Impact Factor (always the 2nd and 3rd columns).

Figure 4.12 *JCR* report for journal *Knowledge Organization*.

(Continued)

"subject areas" includes "Computer science" with 426 cited works. A further limit with the term "information systems" reduces the result to 287 cited works, more than twice the size of the result set in *WoS*. Figure 4.16 shows this result.

Each cited work has a complete reference, with links to source documents; the display can be set to show abstracts. The result set has been sorted by publication date, most recent first. We can adjust the sort order to sort by oldest date, cited by, relevance, first author or source title. Figure 4.17 shows the first screen of the result sorted by "cited by."

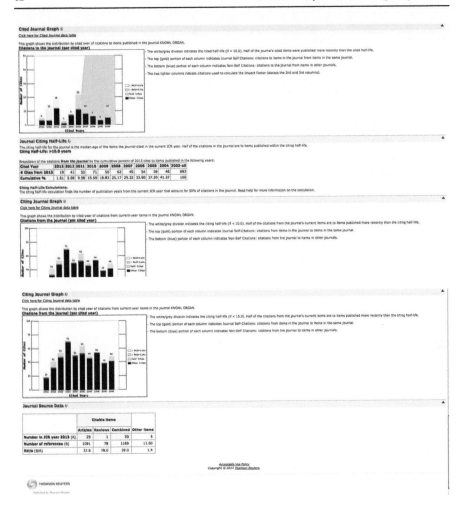

Figure 4.12 Continued.

Basic results are apparent from the full screen. There are 287 documents, of which 159 are conference papers and 106 are journal articles. Computer science is the most populous subject area, the most cited authors are named but receive relatively few citations, and so forth. Each partial result in the boxes at the left can be displayed more fully. We can click on "analyze search results" to receive a visual analysis; this is shown in Figures 4.18 and 4.19.

As before we may display a full record for a specific document. Figure 4.20 is the *Scopus* display for the same document by Gorraiz that we saw in *WoS*. It is interesting to note that the article by Gorraiz and Schloegel was the top-cited paper in the *WoS* result, but is not in the top tier of the *Scopus* result, clearly indicating how different the result sets must be. A domain-analytical study would need to

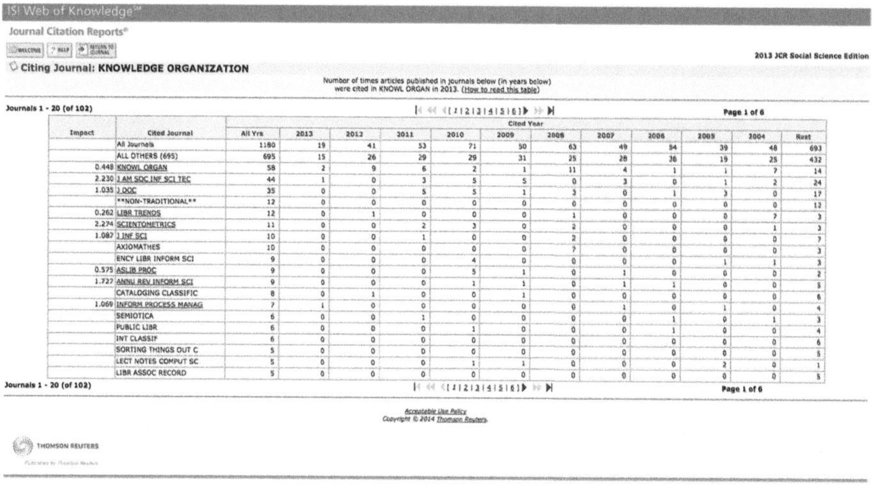

ISI Web of Knowledge℠

Journal Citation Reports®

WELCOME ? HELP RETURN TO JOURNAL

2013 JCR Social Science Edition

Citing Journal: KNOWLEDGE ORGANIZATION

Number of times articles published in journals below (in years below) were cited in KNOWL ORGAN in 2013. (How to read this table)

Journals 1 - 20 (of 102) [1 | 2 | 3 | 4 | 5 | 6] Page 1 of 6

Impact	Cited Journal	All Yrs	Cited Year 2013	2012	2011	2010	2009	2008	2007	2006	2005	2004	Rest
	All Journals	1180	19	41	53	71	50	63	49	54	39	48	693
	ALL OTHERS (695)	695	15	26	29	29	31	25	28	36	19	25	432
0.448	KNOWL ORGAN	58	2	9	6	2	1	11	4	1	1	7	14
2.230	J AM SOC INF SCI TEC	44	1	0	3	5	5	0	3	0	1	2	24
1.035	J DOC	35	0	0	5	5	1	3	0	1	3	0	17
	NON-TRADITIONAL	12	0	0	0	0	0	0	0	0	0	0	12
0.262	LIBR TRENDS	12	0	1	0	0	0	1	0	0	0	7	3
2.274	SCIENTOMETRICS	11	0	0	2	3	0	2	0	0	0	1	3
1.087	J INF SCI	10	0	0	1	0	0	2	0	0	0	0	7
	AXIOMATHES	10	0	0	0	0	0	7	0	0	0	0	3
	ENCY LIBR INFORM SCI	9	0	0	0	4	0	0	0	0	1	1	3
0.575	ASLIB PROC	9	0	0	0	5	1	0	1	0	0	0	2
1.727	ANNU REV INFORM SCI	9	0	0	0	1	1	0	1	1	0	0	5
	CATALOGING CLASSIFIC	8	0	1	0	0	1	0	0	0	0	0	6
1.069	INFORM PROCESS MANAG	7	1	0	0	0	0	0	1	0	1	0	4
	SEMIOTICA	6	0	0	1	0	0	0	0	1	0	1	3
	PUBLIC LIBR	6	0	0	0	1	0	0	0	1	0	0	4
	INT CLASSIF	6	0	0	0	0	0	0	0	0	0	0	6
	SORTING THINGS OUT C	5	0	0	0	0	0	0	0	0	0	0	5
	LECT NOTES COMPUT SC	5	0	0	0	1	1	0	0	0	2	0	1
	LIBR ASSOC RECORD	5	0	0	0	0	0	0	0	0	0	0	5

Journals 1 - 20 (of 102) [1 | 2 | 3 | 4 | 5 | 6] Page 1 of 6

Acceptable Use Policy

Copyright © 2014 Thomson Reuters.

THOMSON REUTERS

Figure 4.13 *JCR* journals citing *Knowledge Organization.*

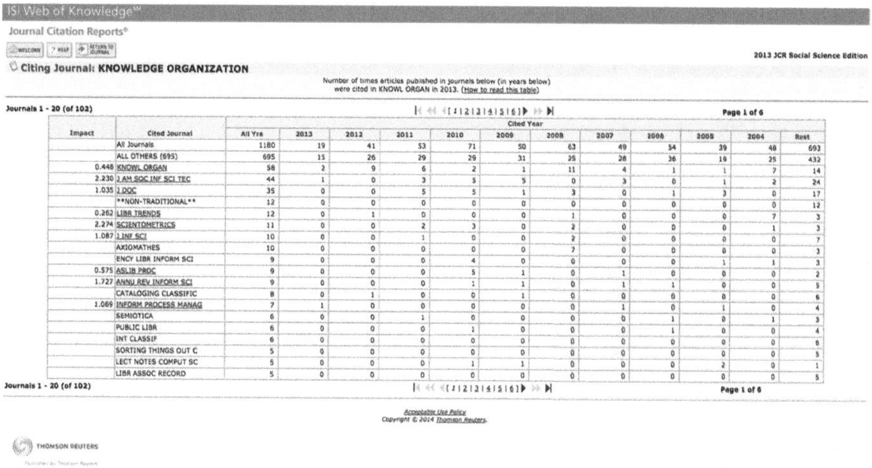

ISI Web of Knowledge℠

Journal Citation Reports®

WELCOME ? HELP RETURN TO JOURNAL

2013 JCR Social Science Edition

Citing Journal: KNOWLEDGE ORGANIZATION

Number of times articles published in journals below (in years below) were cited in KNOWL ORGAN in 2013. (How to read this table)

Journals 1 - 20 (of 102) [1 | 2 | 3 | 4 | 5 | 6] Page 1 of 6

Impact	Cited Journal	All Yrs	Cited Year 2013	2012	2011	2010	2009	2008	2007	2006	2005	2004	Rest
	All Journals	1180	19	41	53	71	50	63	49	54	39	48	693
	ALL OTHERS (695)	695	15	26	29	29	31	25	28	36	19	25	432
0.448	KNOWL ORGAN	58	2	9	6	2	1	11	4	1	1	7	14
2.230	J AM SOC INF SCI TEC	44	1	0	3	5	5	0	3	0	1	2	24
1.035	J DOC	35	0	0	5	5	1	3	0	1	3	0	17
	NON-TRADITIONAL	12	0	0	0	0	0	0	0	0	0	0	12
0.262	LIBR TRENDS	12	0	1	0	0	0	1	0	0	0	7	3
2.274	SCIENTOMETRICS	11	0	0	2	3	0	2	0	0	0	1	3
1.087	J INF SCI	10	0	0	1	0	0	2	0	0	0	0	7
	AXIOMATHES	10	0	0	0	0	0	7	0	0	0	0	3
	ENCY LIBR INFORM SCI	9	0	0	0	4	0	0	0	0	1	1	3
0.575	ASLIB PROC	9	0	0	0	5	1	0	1	0	0	0	2
1.727	ANNU REV INFORM SCI	9	0	0	0	1	1	0	1	1	0	0	5
	CATALOGING CLASSIFIC	8	0	1	0	0	1	0	0	0	0	0	6
1.069	INFORM PROCESS MANAG	7	1	0	0	0	0	0	1	0	1	0	4
	SEMIOTICA	6	0	0	1	0	0	0	0	1	0	1	3
	PUBLIC LIBR	6	0	0	0	1	0	0	0	1	0	0	4
	INT CLASSIF	6	0	0	0	0	0	0	0	0	0	0	6
	SORTING THINGS OUT C	5	0	0	0	0	0	0	0	0	0	0	5
	LECT NOTES COMPUT SC	5	0	0	0	1	1	0	0	0	2	0	1
	LIBR ASSOC RECORD	5	0	0	0	0	0	0	0	0	0	0	5

Journals 1 - 20 (of 102) [1 | 2 | 3 | 4 | 5 | 6] Page 1 of 6

Acceptable Use Policy

Copyright © 2014 Thomson Reuters.

THOMSON REUTERS

Figure 4.14 *JCR* journals cited in *Knowledge Organization.*

compare the two result sets carefully. Alternatively, the two sets could be used together to generate a specific document set for analysis in both databases. The analytical links may be used to generate visualizations of citation analyses related only to this source document. We also may find a record for the author "Gorraiz, J." This is shown in Figure 4.21. As we see, it is possible from this result page to generate various citation analyses related to this single author.

In *Scopus*, journal results are available from the initial search screen by selecting "source title" from the search pull-down menu. Figure 4.22 is the result for the journal

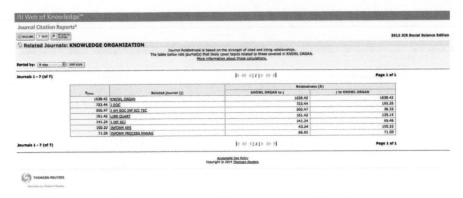

Figure 4.15 *JCR* journals related to *Knowledge Organization*.

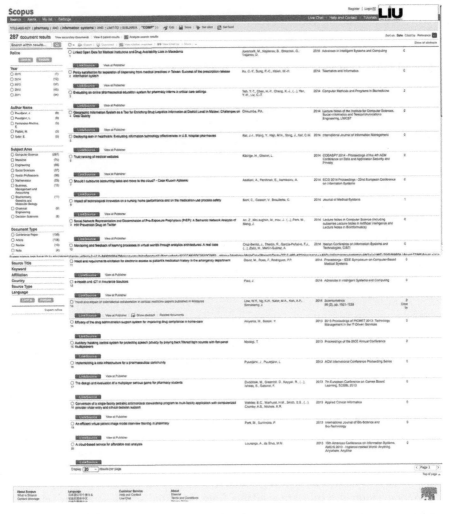

Figure 4.16 *Scopus* subject search "Pharmacy AND information systems limited to Computer science."

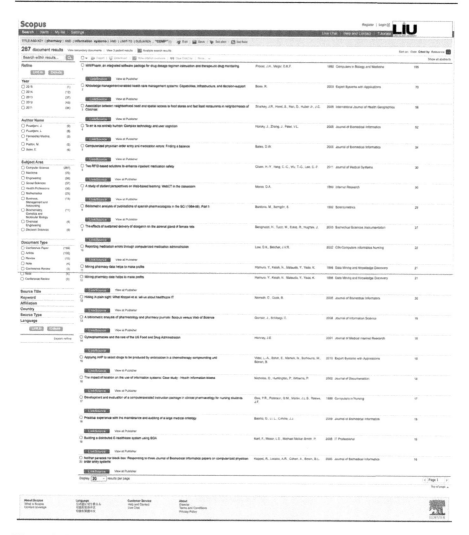

Figure 4.17 *Scopus* subject search "Pharmacy AND information systems limited to Computer science" in "Cited by" order.

Knowledge Organization. Figure 4.23 shows some of the journal metrics available from *Scopus.*

Both *WoS* and *Scopus* represent major steps forward in our ability to analyze domain knowledge using source documents and their citations. The coexistence of the two different databases presents domain analysis with the challenge and opportunity to compare and contrast the results for a richer understanding of domain evolution.

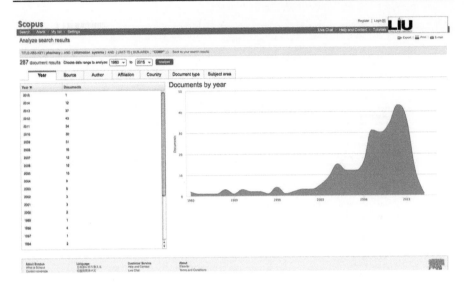

Figure 4.18 *Scopus* result analysis documents by year.

Figure 4.19 *Scopus* search results analyzed documents by author.

4.3 Evidentiary sources for citation analysis: Manual indexing

Unfortunately, many of the domains of interest for knowledge organization domain analysis are not indexed by either service, or are indexed only selectively. This means that researchers often must create manual indexes for citation analysis. Manual

Figure 4.20 *Scopus* record for article by Gorriz and Scholegel.

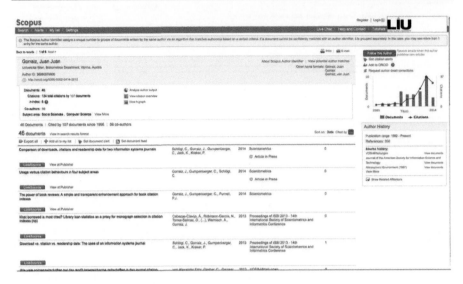

Figure 4.21 *Scopus* author search result for "Gorraiz, J."

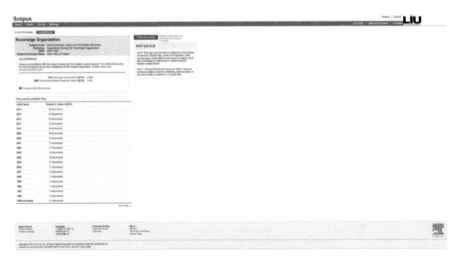

Figure 4.22 *Scopus* result for source title *Knowledge Organization*.

indexing can be easily accomplished by pasting references from digitized source documents into spreadsheets. Once cleaned, the data can be easily manipulated or exported to analytical software packages for more detailed analysis. The central problem in manual indexing, apart from the obvious labor, is the messiness of the data, which must be "cleaned." Many conferences no longer require (or at least no longer enforce) specific referencing guidelines. Also, a large variety of approaches exist to referencing ranging from the minimalist American Psychological Association style to

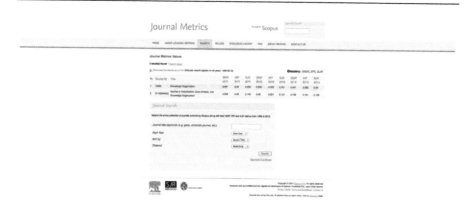

Figure 4.23 *Scopus* journal metrics for *Knowledge Organization*.

the detailed and precise *Chicago Manual of Style* author–date system. Chicago author–date references are easily delimited for indexing. APA references are the most difficult to use for domain analysis because they use many abbreviations that result in imprecision. Proceedings with mixed styles must be converted to one before they can be delimited and cleaned. Unfortunately, it is unlikely that the diverse scientific communities will ever select a single citation style. Online systems that purport to convert references from one style to another do so without the luxury of filling in abbreviated names or titles, which also renders the results difficult.

The proceedings of ISKO biennial international conferences (indeed, many conferences) are not indexed by *Web of Science*, but they do provide documentation on the evolution of the domain at regular intervals. Here as an example of manual indexing Figures 4.24–4.26 show segments of Excel spreadsheets prepared for the analysis of the proceedings (Babik, 2014) of the recent 2014 conference in Krakow. ISKO international proceedings are indexed by *Scopus*, although 2014 had not yet been indexed at the time this text was being written.

In this case, the references from paper to paper were not formatted consistently, which meant that quite a lot of reformatting was necessary. For example, some publication dates were delimited with periods, others with parentheses, and still others were misplaced at the end of the citations. As noted, cleaning the data is time consuming, but necessary to generate useful results.

4.4   Citation analysis of a domain

4.4.1   Geopolitical influences and other demographics

In the conclusion to Chapter 3, we considered that domain-analytical research is centered in the first instance on questions of domain coherence. That is, even before we begin to consider how to discover or extract a common ontology from a domain we

Theme	Title	Country of first author	mean age of work cited	Number of references		Theme	mean age of work cited	Number of references
Current Global Problems in Knowledge Organization			18.81393983	23.75		Current Global Problems in	18.3	23.7
	Classical databases and knowledge organiz	Denmark	0	N/A		Knowledge Organization Do	16.3	20.6
	Knowledge Organization and the Technolo	USA	40.76470588	17		Methods of Knowledge Org	13.8	10.5
	Knowledge Organization for Learning	USA	19.78947368	19		Knowledge Organization Sy	18.7	18.7
	Big Data and Knowledge Extracting to Auto	Germany	10.10526316	19		Knowledge Organization To	12.2	10.5
	Sociological aspects of knowledge and kno	Germany	23.41025641	40		Knowledge Organization To	28.8	14.6
Knowledge Organization Domain and Epistemology			16.26481187	20.875		Knowledge Organization To	9.6	15.5
	Science of Consciousness as a Domain: Issu	India		6		Automatic classification syst	17.3	13.5
	Skepticism and Knowledge Organisation	Canada	9.68421053	19		Knowledge Organization an	12.5	19.5
	Knowledge in Social Memory: empirical ed	Brazil	11.86666667	15		Knowledge Organization for	11.6	16
	The actual role of metaphors in knowledge	Poland	20.375	8		Knowledge Organization for	7.9	14.3
	Integrative Levels of Knowing: An Organiz	Germany	19.33333333	45		Knowledge Organization for	13.5	12.2
	Categories in Knowledge Organization	Brazil		25.5	16		Knowledge Organization Tol	6.4	16.8
	Digital as a Hypsimonic Medium for Epister	Spain		26.94444444	18				
	The Conceptual Dimension of knowledge	Brazil		10.575	40				
Methods of Knowledge Organization			13.86729497	10.5				
	Facets of Facet Analysis: A Theoretical Analysi	India	11.28571429	7				
	Race & Ethnicity in the Encyclopedia of Mi	USA	3.66666667	6				
	The Human Life as Warrant: A Facet Analy	Canada	9.5	10				
	Boundaries and overlaps of disciplines in K	Italy	41.8	15				
	Contours of Knowledge: Caro and Granville	USA	6.88888889	9				
	Art images and Mental Associations: A Pre	Taiwan	10.0625	16				
Knowledge Organization Systems (KOS)			18.72114932	13.75				
	Epistemological and Methodological Criter	USA	21.35294118	17				
	Categories and the Architectonics of Syste	USA	25.15789474	19				
	Facet Detection Using WorldCat and Word	USA	22.81818182	11				
	Classification Interaction Demonstrated Fr	USA	5.53555556	9				
Knowledge Organization Tools: Thesauri			12.23626974	10.5				
	Mapping between ARTstor terms and the	USA	15.61538462	13				
	A More Effective Web Search through Dev	Iran	8.85714285714	8				
Knowledge Organization Tools: Classifications			28.8736369	14.6666667				
	Webs of "Wirkung" modeling the interco	UK	30.15384615	13				
	Classificatory Structure and the Evaluation	USA	54.6	20				
	Towards a Typology of Warrant for 21st Ce	Canada	27.81818182	12				
	Load Bearing or Levittown? The Edifice Me	USA	20.5	12				
	Medical Discourse's Epistemic Influence in	USA	35.625	16				
	Challenges of Facet analysis and Concept F	Croatia	22.41176471	18				
	Hungarians in the history of the UDC	Hungary	41.36363636	12				
	Everyday life classification processes and t	Canada	10.36363636	12				
	Including Knowledge Domains from the ICD	Germany	16.66666667	15				
Knowledge Organization Tools: Taxonomy, Ontologies, Terminology			9.629623606	15.5714286				
	Developing A Taxonomy to Support User B	Singapore	4.75	8				
	Highly Expressive Tagging for Knowledge O	India	7.66666667	10				
	Ontologies and the exchange of technical	Spain	4.57142857	7				
	Music domain analysis for building faceted	India	16.30434783	23				
	Towards a synthetic approach for classifyin	Brazil	11.44	25				
	Terminology as a picture of knowledge org	Poland	9.41176470	17				
	Gottlob Frege's Theory of Definition as Use	Poland	33.26315789	19				
Automatic classification systems			17.53472222	12.5				
	The use of noun phrases in information retrieval: proposing a mechanism for automatic classification	Brazil	16.44444444	9				
	Noun Phrases in Automatic Indexing: a Structural Analysis of the Distribution of Relevant Terms in Doctoral Theses	Brazil	18.625	16				
Knowledge Organization and Representation for IRS			12.53918101	18.5				
	Bias in subject representation: convergences and divergences in the international literature	Brazil	10.13793103	29				
	Information retrieval support: visualisation	Poland	10.1875	16				
	Genetic, intertextuality, and knowledge O	UK	20.54545455	14				
	Consensus Analysis on the development of	Brazil	22.93333333	15				
	Switching Languages and the National Content Consortiums: An Overview on the Challenges of Designing an Iranian Model	Iran	10	8				
	A Baseline Model for Relating Users' Requi	Nigeria	4.84615384	37				
	Using the concepts of Case Based Reasoni	Nigeria	18.55555556	9				
	User-Generated Genre Tags Through the L	USA		33				
	Investigation of levels of abstraction in us	USA	10.31034483	29				
	Faceted navigation in search and discovery	Poland	5.46666667	16				
	Numerical training for the information retr	France	6.26666667	15				
	The treatment of theatrical text content a	Brazil	18.61538462	24				
Knowledge Organization for Special Domain			11.65553752	16				
	Older Adults and eHealth Literacy: Challen	USA	14.27272727	22				
	Organizing and Representing Geographic I	USA	10.26666667	15				
	Knowledge Organisation for the System of	Poland	4.125	8				
	Model of scientific publishing as knowledg	Poland	13.45454545	22				
	Bibliographic subject headings as access p	Finland	18.23428571	14				
	Smart Cities and Knowledge Organization	Poland	8.6	15				
Knowledge Organization for Libraries			7.94818371	14.3333333				
	Bridging the Gaps between Knowledge Org	France	5.06666667	18				
	Digital libraries and semantic searching	Italy	13.61904762	18				
	Using a Semantic Analysis Tool to Generat	USA	11.05882353	17				
	Extending the "Explore" User Task Beyond	USA	8.73333333	15				
	Towards continuous improvement of user	Poland	3.11111111	10				
	Evaluating Discovery tools in Portuguese a	Spain	6.1	10				
Knowledge Organization Education			13.55744049	12.25				
	KO and classification education in the light	Canada	12.09090909	11				
	Knowledge organisation in a digital learnin	Poland	4.88888889	9				
	Characteristics of Library Science Terminol	Mexico	11	20				
	Documentation as Knowledge Organizatio	Brazil	26.25	9				
Knowledge Organization History and Future			6.48333333	16.8				
	Twenty Years After: Scientific Research in the Field of Knowledge Organization in Romania (1993-2012)	Romania	8.4	5				
	Exploring the boundaries of knowledge or	Spain	7.06666667	15				
	Classifications and interdisciplinarity withi	Poland	8.375	17				
	Semantization and standardisation – coupl	Poland	4.2	40				
	Promotion of knowledge on the internatio	Poland	4.375	7				

Figure 4.24 Manual indexing: ISKO 2014 proceedings papers in conference order.

must consider whether we have a coherent and functioning domain. One way to begin answering the question of who belongs to a domain and what activities fall within their common purview is to generate basic demographic data about participants and their work in the domain. Initial metrics can be used to define the parameters of the domain in the same way demographics define a population. As an example, we can continue to look at metrics produced for the analysis of the 2014 ISKO conference that were reported in Smiraglia (2014). ISKO is an international scientific organization, and

1	13th International ISKO Conference, Krakow, Poland, 19-22 May, 2014						
2	*Proceedings*						
3							
4	Theme	Author(s)	Title	Country of first author	mean age of work cited	Number of referenc	Notes (affiliation)
5	Current Global Problems in Knowledge Organization						
6		Birger Hjørland	Classical databases and kno	Denmark	0	N/A	Royal School of Library and Information Science, Copenhagen, Denmark
7		Michael K. Buckland	Knowledge Organization and	USA	40.76470588	17	School of Information, University of California, Berkeley, USA
8		Dagobert Soergel	Knowledge Organization for	USA	19.78947368	19	Department of Library and Information Studies, Graduate School of Education, University at Buffalo, Buffalo, USA
9		Bruno Jacobfeuerborn	Big Data and Knowledge Ext	Germany	10.10526316	19	Deutsche Telekom AG, Bonn, Germany
10		H. Peter Ohly	Sociological aspects of know	Germany	23.41025641	40	President ISKO, Bonn, Germany
11	Knowledge Organization Domain and Epistemology						
12		A.Neelameghan, K. S.	Science of Consciousness as	India	6	6	Sarada Ranganathan Endowment for Library Science, Bangalore, India
13		Rick Szostak	Skepticism and Knowledge O	Canada	9.684210526	19	Department of Economics, University of Alberta, Edmonton, Canada
14		Vera Dodebei, Evelyn	Knowledge in Social Memor	Brazil	11.86666667	15	Federal University of the State of Rio de Janeiro - UNIRIO, Rio de Janeiro, Brazil
15		Marek Hetma ski	The actual role of metaphor	Poland	20.375	8	Faculty of Philosophy and Sociology, Marie Curie-Skłodowska University, Lublin, Poland
16		Michael Kleineberg	Integrative Levels of Knowin	Germany	19.33333333	45	Berlin School of Library and Information Science, Humboldt University, Berlin, Germany
17		Gercina Angela Boren	Categories in Knowledge Or	Brazil	25.5	16	School of Information Science, Federal University of Minas Gerais (UFMG), Belo Horizonte/MG, Brazil
18		Rosa San Segundo Ma	Digital as a Hegemonic Medi	Spain	26.94444444	18	Facultad de Filosofía y Letras, Universidad Carlos III de Madrid, Madrid, Spain
19		José Augusto Guimarã	The Conceptual Dimension c	Brazil	10.575	40	Sao Paulo State University, UNESP, Marília, Brazil
20	Methods of Knowledge Organization						
21		K. S. Raghavan, I. K. Ra	Facets of Facet Analysis: A D	India	11.28571429	7	Centre for Knowledge Analytics&Ontological Engineering (KAnOE), PES Institute of Technology, Bangalore, India
22		Ann M. Graf, Richard	Race & Ethnicity in the Ency	USA	3.666666667	6	School of Information Studies, University of Wisconsin, Milwaukee, USA
23		D. Grant Campbell	The Human Life as Warrant:	Canada	9.5	10	School of Information and Media Studies, University of Western Ontario, London, ON, Canada
24		Claudio Gnoli	Boundaries and overlaps of (	Italy	41.8	15	University of Pavia, Italy
25		Jihee Beak, Richard P.	Contours of Knowledge: Cor	USA	6.888888889	9	School of Information Studies, University of Wisconsin, Milwaukee, USA
26		Shu-Jiun Chen, and Hu	Art Images and Mental Asso	Taiwan	10.0625	16	Institute of Taiwan History, Academia Sinica, Taiwan
27	Knowledge Organization Systems (KOS)						
28		Thomas M. Dousa, Fid	Epistemological and Method	USA	21.35294118	17	Graduate School of Library and Information Science, University of Illinois, Urbana-Champaign, USA
29		Thomas M. Dousa	Categories and the Architect	USA	25.15789474	18	Graduate School of Library and Information Science, University of Illinois, Urbana-Champaign, USA
30		Rebecca Green	Facet Detection Using Word	USA	22.81818182	11	OCLC Online Computer Library Center, Inc., Silver Spring, MD, USA
31		Richard P. Smiraglia	Classification Interaction De	USA	5.555555556	9	School of Information Studies, University of Wisconsin, Milwaukee, USA
32	Knowledge Organization Tools: Thesauri						
33		Jae-wook Ahn, Dagob	Mapping between ARTstor t	USA	15.61538462	13	Graduate School of Education, University at Buffalo, Buffalo, USA
34		Sholeh Arastoopoor, S	A More Effective Web Searc	Iran	8.857142857	8	Regional Information Center for Science and Technology, Shiraz, Iran
35	Knowledge Organization Tools: Classifications						
36		Deborah Lee	Webs of "Wirkung": modelli	UK	30.15384615	15	City University London, UK
37		Thomas M. Dousa	Classificatory Structure and	USA	54.6	20	Graduate School of Library and Information Science, University of Illinois, Urbana-Champaign, USA
38		Lynne C. Howarth, Eva	Towards a Typology of Warr	Canada	27.81818182	12	Faculty of Information Studies, University of Toronto, Toronto, Canada
39		Joseph T. Tennis	Load Bearing or Levittown?	USA	20.5	12	Information School, University of Washington, Seattle, USA
40		Melodie J. Fox	Medical Discourse's Epistem	USA	35.625	16	University of Wisconsin, Milwaukee, USA
41		Ana Vukadin, Aida Sla	Challenges of Facet analysis	Croatia	22.41176471	18	National and University Library Zagreb, Croatia
42		Agnes Hajdu Barát	Hungarians in the history of	Hungary	41.36363636	12	Eötvös Loránd University (ELTE), Budapest, Hungary
43		Jill McTavish	Everyday life classification p	Canada	10.36363636	12	University of Western Ontario, London, Ontario, Canada
44		Ernesto William De Lu	Including Knowledge Domai	Germany	16.66666667	15	Department of Information Sciences, University of Applied Sciences, Potsdam, Germany
45	Knowledge Organization Tools: Taxonomy, Ontologies, Terminology						
46		Christopher S.G. Khoo	Developing A Taxonomy to S	Singapore	4.75	8	Wee Kim Wee School of Communication and Information, Nanyang Technological University, Singapore
47		Kavi Mahesh	Highly Expressive Tagging fo	India	7.666666667	10	Centre for Knowledge Analytics&Ontological Engineering (KAnOE), PES Institute of Technology, Bangalore, India
48		Ricardo Eito-Brun	Ontologies and the exchange	Spain	4.571428571	7	Universidad Carlos III de Madrid, Madrid, Spain
49		Devika P. Madalli, B. R	Music domain analysis for b	India	16.30434783	23	Documentation Research and Training Center (DRTC), Indian Statistical Institute (ISI), Bangalore, India
50		Rodrigo De Santis, Ro	Towards a synthetic approa	Brazil	11.44	25	Brazilian Institute of Information in Science and Technology (IBICT) and Federal University of Rio de Janeiro (UFRJ), Brazil
51		Jadwiga Wo niak-Kasp	Terminology as a picture of	Poland	9.411764706	17	Institute of Information Science and Book Studies, University of Warsaw, Warsaw, Poland
52		Gabriela Besler, Jolant	Gottlob Frege'sTheory of De	Poland	13.26315789	19	University of Silesia in Katowice, Poland
53	Automatic classification systems						
54		Agnaldo Lopes Martin	The use of noun phrases in information retrieval: proposing a mechanism for automatic classification	Brazil	16.44444444	9	Federal University of Minas Gerais, Brazil
55		Luiz Antônio Lopes M	Noun Phrases in Automatic Indexing: a Structural Analysis of the Distribution of Relevant Terms in Doctoral Theses	Brazil	18.625	16	
56	Knowledge Organization and Representation for IRS						
57		Suellen Oliveira Milan	Bias in subject representation: convergences and divergences in the international literature	Brazil	10.13793103	29	São Paulo State University- UNESP, Brazil
58		Hanna Batorowska, B	Information retrieval suppor	Poland	10.1875	16	Pedagogical University in Cracow, Poland
59		Pauline Rafferty	Genette, intertextuality, and	UK	20.54545455	14	Department of Information Studies, Aberystwyth University, UK
60		Juliane Assis, Maria A	Consensus Analysis on the d	Brazil	22.93333333	15	School of Information Science, Universidade Federal de Minas Gerais (UFMG), Belo Horizonte - MG, Brazil
61		Sayyed Mahdi Taheri,	Switching Languages and the National Content Consortiums: An Overview on the Challenges of Designing an Iranian Model	Iran	10	8	Knowledge and Information Sciences Department, AllamehTabatabe'i University, Teheran Iran
62		Bernard Ijesunor Akhi	A Baseline Model for Relatin	Nigeria	4.846153846	37	Department of Computer Science and Engineering, Obafemi Awolowo University, Ile-Ife, Nigeria
63		Olubunmi Akerele, An	Using the concepts of Case B	Nigeria	18.55555556	9	University of Ibadan, Ibadan, Nigeria
64		Hajibayova Lala, Jacob	User-Generated Genre Tags	USA		32	School of Library and Information Science, Indiana University Bloomington, USA
65		Hajibayova Lala, Jacob	Investigation of levels of abs	USA	10.31034483	29	School of Library and Information Science, Indiana University Bloomington, USA
66		Katarzyna Materska	Faceted navigation in search	Poland	5.466666667	16	Cardinal Stefan Wysz ski University Library, Warsaw, Poland
67		Sahbi Sidhom	Numerical training for the in	France	6.266666667	15	LORIA & University of Lorraine, Vandoeuvre, France
68		Verônica Silva Rodrigu	The treatment of theatrical	Brazil	18.61538462	14	Department of Library and Documentation Science, University of São Paulo, São Paulo, Brazil
69	Knowledge Organization for Special Domain						
70		Hemalata Iyer, Mary G	Older Adults and eHealth Lit	USA	14.27272727	22	Department of Information Studies, College of Computing and Information, University at Albany, State University of New York, USA
71		Heather Lea Moulaiso	Organizing and Representing	USA	10.26666667	15	University of Missouri, Missouri, USA
72		Wiesław Babik	Knowledge Organization for	Poland	4.125	8	Institute of Information and Library Science, Jagiellonian University in Kraków, Poland
73		Marek Nahotko	Model of scientific publishin	Poland	13.45454545	22	Institute of Information and Library Science, Jagiellonian University in Kraków, Poland
74		Pekka Henttonen	Bibliographic subject headin	Finland	18.21428571	14	School of Information Sciences, University of Tampere, Finland
75		Diana Pietruch-Reizes	Smart Cities and Knowledge	Poland	9.6	15	Institute of Information and Library Science, Jagiellonian University in Kraków, Poland
76	Knowledge Organization for Libraries						
77		Widad Mustafa El Had	Bridging the Gaps between	France	5.066666667	15	University of Lille 3 Laboratoire Gerlico, France
78		Maria Teresa Biagetti	Digital libraries and semanti	Italy	13.61904762	19	Sapienza Rome University, Rome, Italy
79		Marcia Lei Zeng, Karen	Using a Semantic Analysis To	USA	11.05882353	17	School of Library and Information Science, Kent State University, Kent, USA
80		Athena Salaba, Marcia	Extending the "Explore" Use	USA	8.733333333	15	School of Library and Information Science, Kent State University, Kent, USA
81		Agnieszka Młodzka-St	Towards continuous improv	Poland	3.111111111	10	Central Institute for Labour Protection, National Research Institute, Warsaw, Poland
82		Blanca Rodríguez Brav	Evaluating Discovery tools in	Spain	6.1	10	Universidad de León, Facultad de Filosofía y Letras, University of León, León, Spain
83	Knowledge Organization Education						
84		Michèle Hudon	KO and classification educat	Canada	12.09090909	11	École de bibliothéconomie et des sciences de l'information, Université de Montréal, Montréal, Canada
85		Aneta Kami ska, Irena	Knowledge organization in a	Poland	4.888888889	9	Institute of Educational Sciences, Jesuit University of Philosophy and Education "Ignatianum", Kraków, Poland
86		Catalina Naumis Peña	Characteristics of Library Sci	Mexico	11	20	Instituto de Investigaciones Bibliotecologicas y de la Information, Ciudad Universitaria, Coyoacan, Mexico
87		Luciana Corts Mendes	Documentation as Knowledg	Brazil	26.25	9	University of São Paulo, São Paulo, Brazil
88	Knowledge Organization History and Future						
89		Victoria Frâncu, Tabit	Twenty Years After: Scientific Research in the Field of Knowledge Organization in Romania (1993-2012)	Romania	8.4	5	"Carol I" Central University Library of Bucharest, Bucharest, Romania
90		Maria J. López-Huerta	Exploring the boundaries of	Spain	7.066666667	15	Faculty of Library and Information Science, University of Granada, Granada, Spain
91		Izabela Kije ska-D bro	Classifications and interdisci	Poland	8.375	17	National Information Processing Institute, Warsaw, Poland
92		Barbara Sosi ska-Kalat	Semantization and standard	Poland	4.2	40	Institute of Information Science and Book Studies, University of Warsaw, Warsaw, Poland
93		Barbara Szczepanows	Promotion of knowledge on	Poland	4.375	7	Central Institute for Labour Protection, National Research Institute, Warsaw, Poland

Figure 4.25 Manual indexing: ISKO 2014 proceedings Including authors and countries of affiliation.

the mix of influential research from different parts of the world is always shifting. Thus, affiliations of the first authors of each paper were used to generate a frequency distribution of countries of origin of contributed papers. These are visualized using percentages in Figure 4.27.

Figure 4.26 Manual indexing: ISKO 2014 proceedings, references from each paper.

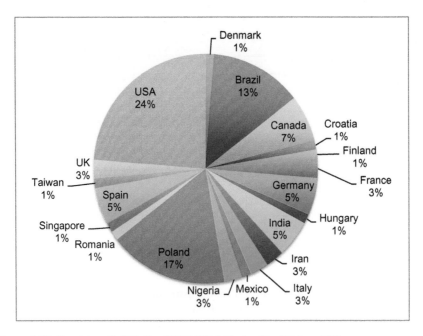

Figure 4.27 Countries of affiliation ISKO 2014 (Smiraglia, 2014, p. 344).

Conference programs often provide general themes for individual panels; these can be recorded and analyzed for conceptual content consistent with the domain's knowledge base. Such lists would not be definitive on their own, but can be used alongside terms extracted from paper titles and abstracts (or texts when possible) for comparison. In analysis of ISKO conferences, it is useful to cross tabulate countries of affiliation with themes to see whether there are any particular geopolitical influences at specific conferences. Comparison can then be made over time using analyses from several successive conferences to demonstrate presence or absence of geopolitical influences.

4.4.2   Citation analysis

Citations themselves provide trace evidence of the social semantics within a scholarly domain, and can be sorted and quantified in a variety of useful ways. The number of references per paper can be indicative of epistemological influences, such as whether the research in the paper is representative of a hard science, a humanistic discipline, or something in between (see Price's Index in Chapter 1). The mean, median, and mode can be reported. In international ISKO conferences usually about half of the papers are humanistic, characterized by large numbers of references to relatively older works, and half scientific (or at least conforming to the norms of IS) with fewer references to recent works. Dates of works cited also can be plotted and used to discover the age of the works in the theoretical background of the domain. Also, dates of works cited can be cross tabulated with geopolitical areas and conference themes to see whether epistemological differences are associated with either influence. Dates can also be used, of course, to calculate half-life, which can be another indicative metric about the epistemological influences in a domain. Dates of cited references from the 2014 ISKO conference ranged from 1873 to 2014, or, the age of works cited ranged from 0 to 141 years. The works cited were fairly recent, which is typical of ISKO conferences; the mean age of works cited was 15.6 years (the median was 8). Histograms were plotted for the distributions of age of cited work and number of references (Figure 4.28)—most papers had between 10 and 20 references, and the age of most works cited peaked around 10 years.

This is consistent with a social-scientific epistemology. ANOVA was used to test the hypothesis that number of references influenced age of cited work; the test indicated there was no statistically significant influence of either variable on the other. Half-life for the domain of the conference was 7.8 years, which is consistent with a social-scientific discipline.

Distribution of media types among the cited references is another indicator of epistemological influences. Hard sciences are more dependent on more immediate publications, usually recent journal articles, while humanistic disciplines are more dependent on older monographic literature. In between, especially in evolving domains, lie technical reports that usually are associated with applied domains, and papers from proceedings; often evolving domains have few or no specific venues for formal publication (or, e.g., have only one small infrequent journal), and thus conference proceedings contain the bulk of research in the domain. Recent evolving

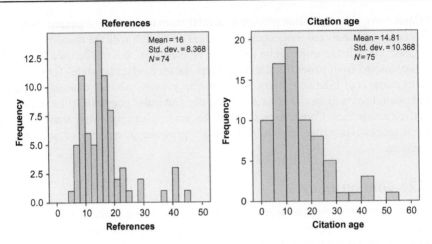

Figure 4.28 Histograms of number of references and citation age (Smiraglia, 2014, p. 346).

domains often have only online proceedings as their formal communication venues. The Dublin Core Metadata Initiative (DCMI) reported by Beak and Smiraglia (2013, 2014) is one such case.

In scientific and social-scientific domains it can be useful to generate a frequency distribution of the most cited journals, again as an indication of the epistemological influences on the domain. The distribution from the 2014 ISKO conference appears in Table 4.1.

These basic metrics are among the demographic indicators that help us understand the parameters of the group, the degree of coherence among its members, and how the group functions epistemologically. All of the metrics in this section were developed manually based on manually indexed proceedings. The same metrics can, of course, be produced quickly using either commercial database. Smiraglia (2013) is a study of the influence of the work of Ranganathan on knowledge organization; the same metrics discussed here are reported in that study based on *Web of Science* features.

4.4.3   *Coword analysis*

Term extraction can be accomplished using relatively simple software. Several programs are available for converting either text snippets or full texts into term lists; Provalis Software's *WordStat* is the program that will be used in this chapter. QSR Internationals *NVivo* also can be used to produce similar analyses. Both software suites are useful for generating term extraction visualizations from qualitative data such as interview narratives. Also, it is possible to accomplish the same task in a rudimentary way by converting all of the spaces in a word processing document into paragraph marks, then sorting the entire file alphabetically, removing stop words (articles, pronouns, etc.) and then creating a frequency distribution of the relatively few words that occur more than once or twice. In other words, it is quite easy to create a simple frequency distribution of words in a text file. Of course, the result is a

Table 4.1 **Most cited journals in ISKO 2014 proceedings**

Journal title	No. citations	%
Knowledge Organization	89	44
Journal of Documentation	23	11
Journal of the American Society for Information Science and Technology	19	9
Information Processing & Management	11	5
Journal of the American Society for Information Science	10	5
Cataloging & Classification Quarterly	8	4
Annual Review of Information Science and Technology	7	3
Cognitive Psychology	6	3
Library Trends	6	3
Aslib Proceedings	5	2
Journal of Information Science	5	2
Library Hi Tech	5	2
The American Archivist	5	2

distribution of words and not of terms, and thus more sophisticated techniques must be employed to isolate term clusters. Nonetheless in much the way a surveyor stands in the meadow on a clear day and looks around to get a sense of the "lay of the land," it makes sense to begin with a simple frequency distribution of words in a text corpus. Table 4.2 is a reproduction of just such a list from the analysis of the 2014 ISKO proceedings.

We can see from the preliminary view that systems, subjects, theories, and semantics are in the top tier, as are more functional terms such as university, libraries, digital, and analysis. Farther down in the distribution (and it is important to remember that we are looking only at the very top tier of a Bradford-like frequency distribution here, a long-tail of singleton words also exists) we see words such as documentation, cognitive, learning, representation, and faceted. This suggests that a term clustering approach might yield metalevel terms such as indexing systems, digital libraries, and semantic analysis, in one cluster, and cognitive approaches and faceted systems might appear in another.

WordStat has a keyword-in-context (KWIC) tool, that we can use to analyze the contexts of the occurrences of the words in this frequency distribution. For example, in Figure 4.29 are screen shots of the first 25 contextual occurrences of "systems" and "theory." "Systems" occurs 50 times and "theory" occurs 48 times in the frequency distribution. The KWIC tool shows us that terms with the word "systems" include "retrieval systems," "information systems," "conceptual systems," "classification systems," and "knowledge organization systems," among others. Terms with the word "theory" include "concept theory" and "activation theory,"

Table 4.2 Most frequently occurring title words in ISKO 2014 proceedings; 50–20 occurrences (Smiraglia, 2014, p. 353)

Word	Frequency	%
Systems	50	2.34
Subject	48	2.24
Theory	48	2.24
University	48	2.24
Libraries	44	2.04
Digital	43	1.99
Semantic	43	1.99
Analysis	42	1.94
Indexing	42	1.94
Technology	38	1.74
Documentation	31	1.39
Study	31	1.39
Cognitive	30	1.34
Search	29	1.29
Approach	28	1.24
Learning	27	1.19
Representation	27	1.19
Faceted	26	1.14
Online	25	1.09
Social	25	1.09
Access	23	0.99
Studies	23	0.99
Review	22	0.94
Using	22	0.94

but most usages of the word "theory" are as a single noun term itself. The drop-down keyword list is included to illustrate the proximity of stem variants such as "theories" or "system," which likewise can be consulted to discover term usages. *WordStat* allows the researcher to use terms gathered from the indexed texts to create a dictionary that can be used as a filter for the term co-occurrence. Figure 4.30 shows a glimpse of a portion of a special dictionary that has been created for use with ISKO proceedings.

This view shows the metalevel terms and stems that can be used to generate multi-dimensionally scaled (MDS) plots for visualization of the term co-occurrence, one aspect of coword analysis. WordStat™ can produce two- or three-dimensional maps to plot the relative position of terms. In Figure 4.31, an MDS plot of the term

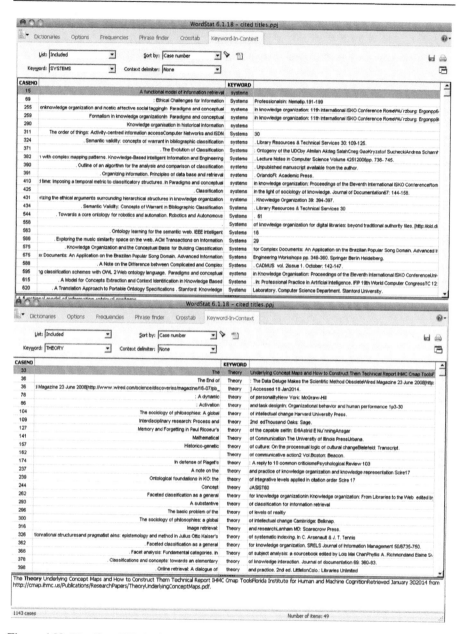

Figure 4.29 *WordStat* KWIC views of "systems" and "theory" and keyword list.

(Continued)

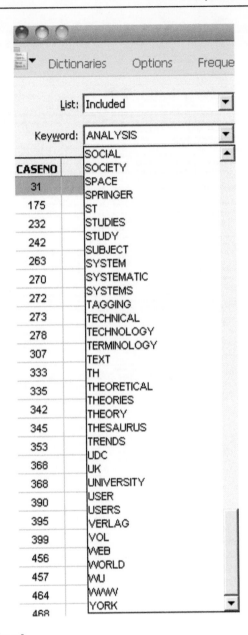

Figure 4.29 Continued.

co-occurrence in the ISKO 2014 proceedings is reproduced. You will see that there are three regions delineated in the illustration; these are indicated in accompanying co-occurrence data. The interpretation of the diagram is reproduced here as well (Smiraglia, 2014, p. 354):

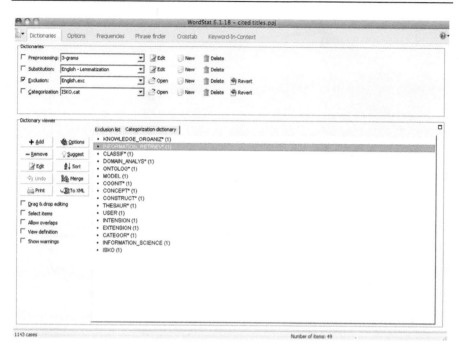

Figure 4.30 *WordStat* with categorization dictionary "ISKO.CAT."

There is a solid core cluster with knowledge organization, classification, concepts, categories, ISKO, and cognition. But behind it is a small cluster with models, and behind both is another cluster where domain analysis and ontology are associated with information science. This suggests that there is, among the contributors to this conference, an ontological discrepancy between concept theory (which is classic KO) and domain analysis, by which concepts are derived, which is perceived rather as closer to information science (IS). Cognition is classic KO, users are IS, but information retrieval models are in their own cluster apart from both.

Goodness of fit statistics are always provided with MDS plots. One seeks low stress (the closer to zero the better) and high R-squared (the closer to one the better) if the model fits the data well. The use of these statistics is addressed by McCain (1990), and White (2003) with regard to cocitation analysis. Notice, however, that even when the model fits the data well it is not necessarily a good representation of reality. When the model does not fit the data well the researcher should adjust the source data, perhaps removing terms with too few occurrences or merging very granular terms into the more general categories to which they belong. This is one of the qualitative aspects of coword analysis, and it involves very detailed understanding of the domain itself. This method is empirical, but is not generalizable beyond the population under study. Notice also the advantage of visualization provided by multidimensional diagrams and by color; in this case, the different colors align with the different language blocks

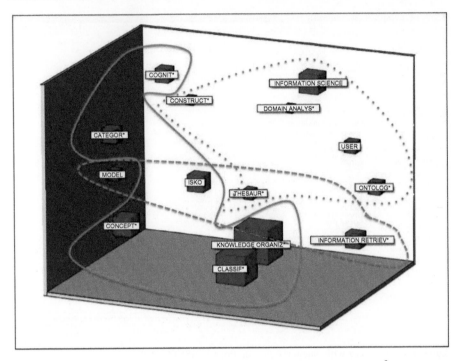

Figure 4.31 *WordStat* MDS plot of frequently used terms (stress $= 0.24256$, $R^2 = 0.8596$) (Smiraglia, 2014, p. 354).

within the keyword list. So we can actually see the comparative impact of the different language contributions to the proceedings under analysis.

These are the basic steps in coword analysis. The level of sophistication of the analysis is entirely dependent of the taxonomic depth of analysis. In this case, only titles of conference papers were used to generate source words and terms. It is possible to use abstracts, and full texts, although problems of scaling must be dealt with in such cases. As a first glimpse of a domain, extraction of terms from titles of conference papers is a good beginning indicator. The frequency distribution included more than 1000 single-word "terms," that likely are indicative of the granularity of the intension of the domain. What we have here is a metalevel indication of the extension of the domain.

It is important to understand that word extraction, or even term extraction, is not the same thing as ontology discovery. That is, the words, or terms, always are used in context, and these statistical methods make it difficult to comprehend the subtleties of context. This is why domain analysis must always involve multiple methods and evoke multitheoretical explanations. For example, there now have been many empirical analyses of ISKO proceedings, but to date there have been no discourse analyses of these same source documents. Discourse analysis could add the contextual subtleties missing from the empirical term extraction techniques for the description of the domain's ontological base.

Figure 4.32 Voyeur word cloud from ISKO 2014 paper titles (Smiraglia, 2014, p. 353).

Voyant is a tool of the *Cirrus* text analysis initiative (http://docs.voyant-tools.org/context/background/). We saw a small example of text analysis from *Voyeur* in Chapter 3. The tool allows you to enter any text in full and generate word frequency analyses and visualizations, which can be manipulated (for instance, stop words can be removed, or generic terms from a particular domain also can be removed to improve precision of representation). For example, the word list and frequencies from the titles of papers in the ISKO 2014 conference proceedings were entered into the Voyant visualization tool. The full result screen is shown in Figure 4.32 (reproduced from Smiraglia 2014, p. 353).

On the *Voyeur* results screen, any word in the visualization may be clicked on to produce a word trends frequency graph, a keyword in context chart showing how the word was used, a term summary, as well as a complete frequency distribution of the words in the corpus. Various language stop lists may be applied to remove articles. Most of the results may be exported as well.

4.4.4 Author cocitation analysis

Author cocitation analysis is based on the idea that if two authors are citing the same material they likely are engaged in similar or comparable research, or at the very least are working in the same domain. Using techniques clearly explained by McCain (1990), and refined by White (2003) author cocitations among the works cited by a domain can be used to generate visualizations of cocited authors. These visualizations represent the view of the domain held by those who cocite these authors. That is, the scholars who are active in the domain cite authors in common who they believe to be somehow similarly engaged in advancing the domain. The technique involves gathering cocitation data into a matrix and then processing it using software that can create

MDS plots based on various co-occurrence statistics. As McCain points out (1990, p. 433), selection of the author set is the most basic step in the process and is closely related to the problems of domain definition. In general, a useful methodological approach is to attempt the analysis with different but overlapping author sets, to see how the domain visualization is, or is not, representative. In much of the research in knowledge organization, lists of prolific authors are used, or are combined with lists of most cited authors (which usually overlap) to generate a beginning author set. Other possibilities are simply to work with all participants at a particular point in time, or in a particular event (such as a conference). Adjusting the list will be necessary because not all authors in a domain are cocited, and many software programs used to generate analyses will not function properly if there are empty cells or cells with low values in the matrix. Thus, the first stage involves some trial and error work on the part of the researcher, whose domain knowledge will be critical. Also, depending on the domain, quickly gathering cocitation data from *WoS* or *Scopus* might or might not be possible. In evolving domains, manual indexing to discover cocitations will frequently be necessary.

McCain (1990) gives a complete list of steps and readers are advised to study her text carefully. Essentially, the process includes searching a corpus for cocitations, entering cocitation totals into a matrix, using software such as IBM-SPSS PASW-Statistics to classify and analyze the data and to produce an MDS plot showing regions or clusters of cocited authors, and then interpreting the result. Figure 4.33 is reproduced from a matrix of author cocitation among the authors of the ISKO 2014 conference papers.

The two diagonal halves of the matrix are the same. The yellow diagonal appears where empty cells would normally occur because authors cannot cocite themselves. As White (2003) explains, the diagonal will not run in many programs if the cells are empty; in this case, author means were entered in each column. The means must be calculated separately and entered manually to keep the spreadsheet from

	Hjørland	Gnoli	Smiraglia	Szostak	Beghtol	López-Huertas	Broughton	Dahlberg	Mai	Olson	Buckland	Tennis	Dousa	McIlwaine	Otlet	Foucault	Ranganathan
Hjørland	2	5	5	3	4	3	3	3	4	1	2	2	2	4	1	1	2
Gnoli	5	2	3	4	3	3	3	1	2	2	1	3	1	2	0	0	3
Smiraglia	5	3	1	1	1	1	2	2	1	0	1	2	1	1	0	0	1
Szostak	3	4	1	1	2	0	0	0	2	1	2	0	1	1	0	0	1
Beghtol	4	4	1	2	1	4	1	0	4	2	3	1	2	2	0	0	1
López-Huertas	3	3	1	0	4	1	0	1	1	1	0	1	0	2	0	0	0
Broughton	3	3	2	0	1	0	0.8	0	0	0	0	0	2	0	0	0	3
Dahlberg	3	1	2	0	0	1	0	0.5	0	0	0	1	0	1	0	0	0
Mai	4	2	1	2	4	1	0	0	1	1	2	1	1	2	0	0	0
Olson	1	2	0	1	2	1	0	0	1	0.7	0	2	0	1	0	1	0
Buckland	2	2	1	2	2	0	0	0	2	0	0.8	0	1	1	0	0	0
Tennis	2	3	2	0	1	1	0	1	1	2	0	0.8	0	0	0	0	0
Dousa	2	1	1	1	2	0	2	0	1	0	1	0	0.7	1	0	0	0
McIlwaine	4	2	1	1	2	2	0	1	2	1	1	0	1	1	0	0	0
Otlet	1	0	0	0	0	0	0	0	0	0	0	0	0	0	0.06	0	0
Foucault	1	0	0	0	0	0	0	0	0	1	0	0	0	0	0	0.1	0
Ranganathan	2	2	1	1	1	0	3	0	0	0	0	0	0	0	0	0	0.6

Figure 4.33 Author cocitation matrix from ISKO 2014 proceedings.

recalculating. An alternative is to use the highest cocitation figure in each column in the diagonal. The MDS plot for this matrix appears in Figure 4.34.

The lines around the clusters are provided using drawing software such as that found in Microsoft Word or PowerPoint. The delineation of the clusters is suggested by co-occurrence statistics that accompany the visualization. Their meaning is always debatable, and is highly dependent on the researcher's domain knowledge. It is always possible, of course, to consult the source documents that were cocited, although the process is laborious and it is not always clear even from the sources why cocitation has occurred. Often interpretation involves considering several perspectives and trajectories from within the domain to arrive at a useful result.

In this case, the solid line surrounds a cluster of highly cited authors in the core of the domain (concept theory) and the other clusters represent segments of the research front (primarily domain analysis and faceted classification techniques). In the source document (Smiraglia, 2014), as in other recent domain analyses of knowledge organization proceedings, this interconference cocitation is paired with a cocitation map of the same author set derived from the *WoS*. The pairing helps demonstrate different perceptions of the domain's knowledge base, and it also serves as a form of data triangulation. When the two visualizations are more or less the same it serves as a form of verification of the core clusters, and where they diverge it demonstrates the evolution of the research front as represented by any particular conference over and against the perceptions of the whole domain as indicated in journal citation captured by the

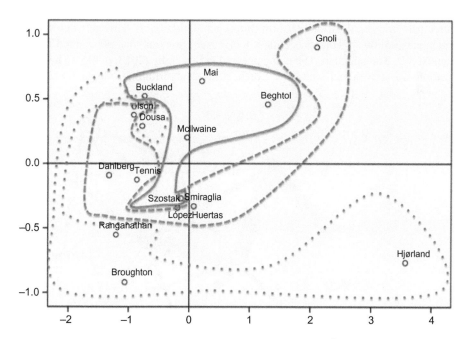

Figure 4.34 Interconference author cocitation (stress = 0.11595, R^2 = 0.96218) (Smiraglia, 2014, p. 352).

WoS. Similarly, the clusters are comparable to but slightly different from those developed using coword analysis shown in Figure 4.31, which also serves as a form of data and methodological triangulation to enrich the visualization of the domain.

Other similarity measures, such as bibliographic coupling and journal cocitation are used in IS to explore the evolution of and communication among and within scholarly domains. However, these techniques, so far, have not been found useful in knowledge organization domain analysis. A possible explanation is that the core research question in knowledge organization has as it focuses the extraction of a domain's knowledge base, rather than its functioning. Recent research on boundary objects—terms used by two neighboring communities to help them intepret each other's research—has begun to demonstrate the potential usefulness of these additional techniques.

4.4.5 Network analysis

Network analysis is a set of techniques derived from network theory, which has evolved from computer science to demonstrate the power of social network influences. Using network analysis in domain analysis can add another layer of methodological triangulation by providing a different way to read and interpret the same data. The use of network analysis in knowledge organization domain analysis is recent and is just evolving. The visualization technique involves mapping relationships among entities based on the symmetry or asymmetry of their relative proximity. For example, the network map in Figure 4.35 was developed using Gephi, an open source network visualization platform (http://gephi.github.io/). This network visualization is based on an author cocitation matrix from research that cites famed Indian scientist S.R. Ranganathan. The map appeared in Smiraglia (2013, p. 715). The visualization was developed using the Force Atlas 2 algorithm in Gephi 0.8.2. The

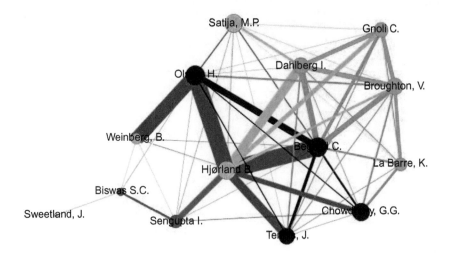

Figure 4.35 Author cocitation network visualized (Smiraglia, 2013, p. 715).

technique involves changing the original matrix into a network file, and then using Gephi to enhance the visualization.

The complexity of the network map helps us visualize the degree of interconnectedness among the thematic clusters represented by cocited authors. Instead of clusters we see network pathways, as though in a street map. We can see, for example, that although everyone is connected in some way in this map, some are only barely connected while others are closely interconnected. The different densities of the connecting edges help us visualize the relative strength of the associations.

Sci2™, the "Science of Science" tool, created by Indiana University's Sci^2 Team (https://sci2.cns.iu.edu) is a tool that can be used to automate much of the work of producing domain visualizations. Domain citation data can be downloaded into Sci2, which can then be used to select and map cocitation data and produce a number of visualizations.

4.4.6 Instantiation networks

Quantifying and analyzing instantiation networks is a way of focusing on conceptual canons in domains by isolating classical works that have taken on a cultural role in a theoretical paradigm. There have been three kinds of instantiation studies to date: (1) those that identify and quantify instantiating works in bibliographic networks such as OCLC's WorldCat or specific library catalogs; (2) those that investigate the extent of instantiation in specific domains, such as theology, American literature, or music; and (3) those that quantify and analyze the nodal structure, and thus the domain-centered change in ideational and semantic content of multiply instantiating progenitor works, such as Bridget of Sweden's *Revelations*. In all three cases the methodology involves constituting the source domain, isolating specific works, and searching bibliographic catalogs and networks for evidence of instantiations, extant or known. The first step, as in all of domain analysis, requires domain expertise and results will vary from study to study, which is why it is critical to document-specific procedures. It is best to use any available list of works in a domain, especially one that is the product of domain activity, such as the annual lists of best sellers used in Smiraglia (2007). It would be appropriate, however, to use individual syllabi, or to collect syllabi from a domain to generate lists of canonical works. Of course, large commercial indexing services can be used to isolate all publications carrying the same domain descriptor, as Marchese (2002) did with works in the domain of American literature, which were extracted from *Books-in-Print* and *Books-out-of-Print* collectively. To date most studies of instantiation have focused on monographic works, which are easily quantified using services such as the OCLC WorldCat. Instantiation is rare among nonmonographic works such as research articles, which only occasionally are reprinted. It would be possible to study ideational instantiation in a domain by using nonmonographic works, as Coleman (2002) did with scientific theories; such studies would be reliant on citation networks to discover, for example, the documentary record of the quotation of a given theory or result.

Instantiation in a domain, as noted earlier, usually follows a power-law distribution, such that approximately one-third or fewer of the works in a domain will be found to have instantiated over time. The obverse then is that the majority of the works in a domain will exist in singleton instantiations. When works are drawn from bibliographic systems such as library catalogs, it is important to make a distinction between bibliographic records, which are the entities in the sampling frame, and the works represented in them, which are the targets for the analysis of instantiation. This means that once a sample of bibliographic records is extracted from a library catalog or bibliographic utility, a second selection process must be used to discover the list of works represented among those bibliographic records, and then to guarantee no work in the sample was selected because of unequal probabilities of representation. The technique for undertaking this task is described in Smiraglia (2001, p. 155).

Once specific works have been identified for analysis, the procedure is simply to search them as widely as possible to identify extant or known instantiations. Two simple examples will serve for demonstration. S.R. Ranganathan's work, *Prologomena to Library Classification*, is a core classical work in knowledge organization that can serve as an example. A search in the OCLC WorldCat reveals 48 bibliographic records; these are shown in Figure 4.36.

As mentioned, it is important to understand that this result shows bibliographic records from many inputting sources, so the nodes in the result need to be isolated. Unfortunately, this usually involves looking at each record individually to be certain unique results have been reported. Nonetheless in this result we have six dates represented—1937, 1957, 1967, 1989, 1990, and 2006. In tabular form the individual instantiations are shown in Table 4.3.

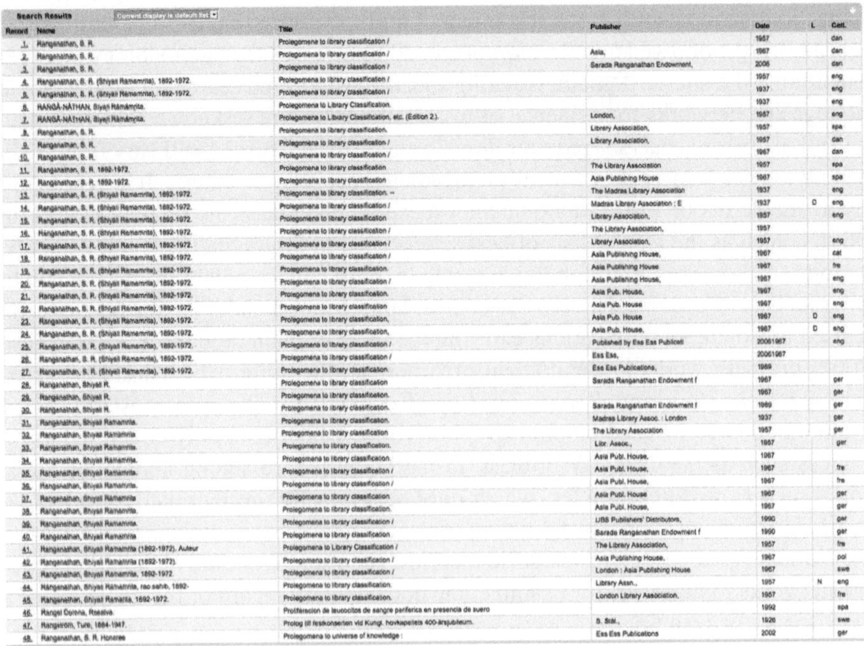
Search Results   Current display is default list

Record	Name	Title	Publisher	Date	L	Catl.
1.	Ranganathan, S. R.	Prolegomena to library classification /		1957		dan
2.	Ranganathan, S. R.	Prolegomena to library classification /	Asia,	1967		dan
3.	Ranganathan, S. R.	Prolegomena to library classification /	Sarada Ranganathan Endowment,	2006		dan
4.	Ranganathan, S. R. (Shiyali Ramamrita), 1892-1972.	Prolegomena to library classification /		1957		eng
5.	Ranganathan, S. R. (Shiyali Ramamrita), 1892-1972.	Prolegomena to library classification /		1937		eng
6.	RANGĀ-NĀTHAN, Siyali Rāmāmṛita.	Prolegomena to Library Classification.		1937		eng
7.	RANGĀ-NĀTHAN, Siyali Rāmāmṛita.	Prolegomena to Library Classification, etc. (Edition 2.).	London,	1957		eng
8.	Ranganathan, S. R.	Prolegomena to library classification.	Library Association,	1957		spa
9.	Ranganathan, S. R.	Prolegomena to library classification /	Library Association,	1957		dan
10.	Ranganathan, S. R.	Prolegomena to library classification /		1967		dan
11.	Ranganathan, S. R. 1892-1972.	Prolegomena to library classification	The Library Association	1957		spa
12.	Ranganathan, S. R. 1892-1972.	Prolegomena to library classification	Asia Publishing House	1967		spa
13.	Ranganathan, S. R. (Shiyali Ramamrita), 1892-1972.	Prolegomena to library classification. --	The Madras Library Association	1937		eng
14.	Ranganathan, S. R. (Shiyali Ramamrita), 1892-1972.	Prolegomena to library classification /	Madras Library Association ; E	1937	D	eng
15.	Ranganathan, S. R. (Shiyali Ramamrita), 1892-1972.	Prolegomena to library classification	Library Association,	1957		eng
16.	Ranganathan, S. R. (Shiyali Ramamrita), 1892-1972.	Prolegomena to library classification /	The Library Association,	1957		
17.	Ranganathan, S. R. (Shiyali Ramamrita), 1892-1972.	Prolegomena to library classification /	Library Association,	1957		eng
18.	Ranganathan, S. R. (Shiyali Ramamrita), 1892-1972.	Prolegomena to library classification /	Asia Publishing House,	1967		cat
19.	Ranganathan, S. R. (Shiyali Ramamrita), 1892-1972.	Prolegomena to library classification.	Asia Publishing House	1967		fre
20.	Ranganathan, S. R. (Shiyali Ramamrita), 1892-1972.	Prolegomena to library classification /	Asia Publishing House,	1967		eng
21.	Ranganathan, S. R. (Shiyali Ramamrita), 1892-1972.	Prolegomena to library classification.	Asia Pub. House,	1967		eng
22.	Ranganathan, S. R. (Shiyali Ramamrita), 1892-1972.	Prolegomena to library classification	Asia Pub. House	1967		eng
23.	Ranganathan, S. R. (Shiyali Ramamrita), 1892-1972.	Prolegomena to library classification,	Asia Pub. House	1967	D	eng
24.	Ranganathan, S. R. (Shiyali Ramamrita), 1892-1972.	Prolegomena to library classification,	Asia Pub. House,	1967	D	eng
25.	Ranganathan, S. R. (Shiyali Ramamrita), 1892-1972.	Prolegomena to library classification /	Published by Ess Ess Publicati	20061967		eng
26.	Ranganathan, S. R. (Shiyali Ramamrita), 1892-1972.	Prolegomena to library classification /	Ess Ess,	20061967		
27.	Ranganathan, S. R. (Shiyali Ramamrita), 1892-1972.	Prolegomena to library classification.	Ess Ess Publications,	1989		
28.	Ranganathan, Shiyali R.	Prolegomena to library classification	Sarada Ranganathan Endowment f	1967		ger
29.	Ranganathan, Shiyali R.	Prolegomena to library classification.		1967		ger
30.	Ranganathan, Shiyali R.	Prolegomena to library classification.	Sarada Ranganathan Endowment f	1989		ger
31.	Ranganathan, Shiyali Ramamrita.	Prolegomena to library classification.	Madras Library Assoc. : London	1937		ger
32.	Ranganathan, Shiyali Ramamrita	Prolegomena to library classification	The Library Association	1957		ger
33.	Ranganathan, Shiyali Ramamrita.	Prolegomena to library classification.	Libr. Assoc.,	1957		ger
34.	Ranganathan, Shiyali Ramamrita.	Prolegomena to library classification.	Asia Publ. House,	1967		
35.	Ranganathan, Shiyali Ramamrita.	Prolegomena to library classification /	Asia Publ. House,	1967		fre
36.	Ranganathan, Shiyali Ramamrita.	Prolegomena to library classification /	Asia Publ. House,	1967		fre
37.	Ranganathan, Shiyali Ramamrita	Prolegomena to library classification	Asia Publ. House	1967		ger
38.	Ranganathan, Shiyali Ramamrita.	Prolegomena to library classification.	Asia Publ. House,	1967		ger
39.	Ranganathan, Shiyali Ramamrita.	Prolegomena to library classification /	UBS Publishers' Distributors,	1990		ger
40.	Ranganathan, Shiyali Ramamrita	Prolegomena to library classification	Sarada Ranganathan Endowment f	1990		ger
41.	Ranganathan, Shiyali Ramamrita (1892-1972). Auteur	Prolegomena to Library Classification /	The Library Association,	1957		fre
42.	Ranganathan, Shiyali Ramamrita (1892-1972).	Prolegomena to library classification /	Asia Publishing House,	1967		pol
43.	Ranganathan, Shiyali Ramamrita, 1892-1972.	Prolegomena to library classification /	London : Asia Publishing House	1967		swe
44.	Ranganathan, Shiyali Ramamrita, rao sahib, 1892-	Prolegomena to library classification.	Library Assn.,	1957	N	eng
45.	Ranganathan, Shiyali Ramarita, 1892-1972.	Prolegomena to library classification.	London Library Association,	1957		fre
46.	Rangel Corona, Rosalva.	Proliferacion de leucocitos de sangre periferica en presencia de suero		1992		spa
47.	Rangstrom, Ture, 1884-1947.	Prolog till festkonserten vid Kungl. hovkapellets 400-årsjubileum.	S. Stål.,	1926		swe
48.	Ranganathan, S. R. Honoree	Prolegomena to universe of knowledge :	Ess Ess Publications	2002		ger

Figure 4.36 OCLC WorldCat result for Ranganathan's Prologomena.

Table 4.3 Instantiations of Ranganathan's *Prologomena*

1937	Madras: Madras Library Association; London: E. Goldston, xvi, 305 pages. Publication series 6
1957	2nd ed. with a preface by W. C. Berwick Sayers. London: Library Association, 1957, 487 pages
1967	Assisted by M.A. Gopinath. 3rd ed. Bombay, New York, Asia Pub. House, 640 pages, Ranganathan series in library science, 20
1989	Microfilm, 3rd ed., repr. Bangalore: Sarada Ranganathan Endowment for Library Science
1990	3rd ed., repr. Bangalore
2006	New Delhi: Published by Ess Ess Publication for Sarada Ranganathan Endowment for Library Science, Bangalore. Reprint of 3rd ed.: London: Asia Pub. House, 1967

There are essentially three nodes, a first edition of 1937, a second edition of 1957, and a third edition of 1967. There are a 1989 microfilm, and 1990 and 2006 reprints of the 1967 edition (Ranganathan, 1967). This is a fairly straightforward instantiation network of derivations. More complexity is, of course, possible, and the more complex the network the more complicated the search for instantiations must become. Another example is the film by Françoise Levie *The Man Who Wanted to Classify the World*, a documentary film about the career of Paul Otlet. Table 4.4 shows the instantiations identified in the WorldCat.

Table 4.4 Instantiations of *The Man Who Wanted to Classify the World*

2002	Videocassette VHS	Brussels, Sofidoc	L'Homme qui voulait classer le monde; Sofidoc, Wild Heart Productions, RTBF (Belgian television)
	English language narration and subtitles		The Man who wanted to classify the World
	English VHS cassette	New York: Filmakers Library	
	Videodisc of NY filmakers		
2003	Videodisc	Nivelles, Belgium: Memento Productions	Dutch title: De man die de wereld in kaart wou brengen
	English, French, and Dutch versions in the package		
2004	Online video in English	New York, NY: Filmakers Library	

Here we have essentially one intellectual entity—a 60-min video recording with narration and subtitles in English, French, and Dutch—which has been repackaged several times. It began as a VHS cassette publication, was republished on videodisc, and then became an online video recording. The product was produced for Belgian television in association with Otlet's archives at the Mundaneum in Mons, Belgium. This means the film, visually identical, is released with narration and subtitles in English, French, and Dutch, all at the same time. Because of the differences in publishing the recording in different playback media, and the mix of languages in the progenitor, the instantiation network manages to be complex despite there being no change in intellectual content.

In both of these simple cases, we have indications of the culture and canon of the domains in which these canonical works instantiate. That means instantiation research contributes one more piece of evidence to the comprehension of a domain that produces information objects that can be analyzed as trace evidence and quantified. As noted previously, instantiation research is still in a nascent stage; researchers are advised to study carefully the reports of prior research, especially in Vellucci (1997) and Smiraglia (2001).

References

Babik, W. (Ed.), 2014. Knowledge organization in the 21st century: between historical patterns and future prospects. Proceedings of the Thirteenth International ISKO Conference, 19–22 May 2014, Kraków, Poland. In: Advances in Knowledge Organization, vol. 14. Ergon Verlag, Würzburg.

Beak, J., Smiraglia, R.P., 2013. With a focused intent: evolution of DCMI as a research community. In: Proceedings of the International Conference on Dublin Core and Metadata Applications, Lisbon, Portugal: DC-2013, pp. 126–134. http://dcpapers.dublincore.org/pubs.

Beak, J., Smiraglia, R.P., 2014. Contours of knowledge: core and granularity in the evolution of the DCMI domain. In: Babik, W. (Ed.), Knowledge Organization in the 21st Century: Between Historical Patterns and Future Prospects. Proceedings of the 13th International ISKO Conference, Krakow, Poland, 19–22 May, 2014. In: Advances in Knowledge Organization, vol. 14. Ergon-Verlag, Würzburg, pp. 136–143.

Coleman, A.S., 2002. Scientific models as works. Cat. Classif. Q. 33 (3/4), 129–159.

Marchese, C., 2002. Works of American literature. Unpublished seminar paper, Long Island University.

McCain, K.W., 1990. Mapping authors in intellectual space: a technical overview. J. Am. Soc. Inf. Sci. 41, 433–443.

Ranganathan, S.R., 1967. Prologomena to Library Classification, Assisted by M.P. Gopinath, third ed. Asia Publishing House, Bombay, New York.

Smiraglia, R.P., 2001. The Nature of a Work: Implications for the Organization of Knowledge. Scarecrow Press, Lanham, MD.

Smiraglia, R.P., 2007. The "works" phenomenon and best selling books. Cat. Classif. Q. 44 (3/4), 179–195.

Smiraglia, R.P., 2013. Prolegomena to a new order: a domain-analytical review of the influence of S.R. Ranganathan on knowledge organization. SRELS J. Inf. Manag. 50 (6), 709–719.

Smiraglia, R.P., 2014. ISKO 13's bookshelf: knowledge organization, the science, thrives—an editorial. Knowl. Organ. 41, 343–356.

Vellucci, S.L., 1997. Bibliographic Relationships in Music Catalogs. Scarecrow Press, Lanham, MD.

White, H.D., 2003. Author co-citation analysis and Pearson's r. J. Am. Soc. Inf. Sci. Technol. 54, 1250–1259.

Qualitative analysis: Cognitive work analysis

5.1 Qualitative methods for domain analysis

In the preceding chapter, we surveyed empirical techniques for analyzing a domain based on trace evidence contained in its source documents. In particular, the use of full texts of formal publications allows the straightforward extraction of term lists that can be used to develop more or less detailed interpretations of a domain's knowledge base. Citation analysis uses the formal record of referencing, which is considered to be a public form of communication among scholars, to generate visualizations of thematic and theoretical clusters in domains. These powerful techniques can yield replicable ontological pictures of the evolution of a domain's knowledge base over time. The methods can be combined to generate more powerful results by incorporating data and methodological triangulation to generate comparable or even divergent interpretations. All of this presents a rich picture of a domain for knowledge organization.

Another set of techniques based on qualitative analysis has been used with good results to analyze the functioning of a domain from an ethnographic perspective. The most recent evolution of the methodology is based on a technique called cognitive work analysis (CWA), generated from the work by Vicente (1999) and Rasmussen et al. (1994). CWA is fairly new in knowledge organization. It incorporates a set of techniques that are derived from qualitative research methods, which in turn are based on the theoretical paradigm of symbolic interaction put forth by Blumer (1969). Symbolic interaction is a social theory based on the notion that all human interaction involves in some way the interpretation of symbols. A simple example can be that of a committee chairperson. The members of a committee sit around a table and all pay attention to one person, who generally sits in front, talks more prominently, acts authoritatively, and therefore is assumed to be in charge. Any stranger walking into a committee meeting can view this interaction and interpret the actions of the person in front symbolically. That person must be in charge because that person seems to be in charge. Symbolic interaction suggests we consider the same phenomenon from a different perspective, which is, the observer reacts symbolically to the authoritative demeanor and behavior, and therefore yields obeisance to the presumed chair. The example is simple, but the consequences of symbolic interaction often are immensely important to the functioning and therefore to the knowledge base and culture of a domain. The purpose of qualitative methods is to gain entry to the symbolic cultural knowledge of the actors in a domain, so as to interpret better the contexts for the concepts in their ontological base.

Domain Analysis for Knowledge Organization

5.2 Cognitive work analysis

The CWA methodology involves research from inside the environment of a domain. The word "work" in the name of the methodology comes from the presumption that the participants in the domain work together in some way. Specific qualitative techniques may be combined in various ways. The researcher should work from inside the work environment so as to participate alongside the domain members. This allows the researcher to understand symbolic interactions taking place among the workers, as well as the opportunity to observe their use of knowledge, taxonomy, and any other elements of knowledge organization. Observation may be unobtrusive or obtrusive, or both. Participant observation may take place by working side by side with domain members, workers may be video recorded for subsequent observation, or structured participant observation may take place by asking participants to work and think aloud while the researcher observes. Focus groups and individual interviews may be added to the mix. Complete narrative analysis often reveals points of symbolic interaction which then can be explained subsequently by the use of grounded theory.

Specifically, CWA makes use of the famous "onion model" to describe its multilayered analytical approach. The onion is reproduced in Figure 5.1. Working from the core out we see actors (domain participants) at the center; analysis of user characteristics means understanding not only the resources used by participants, but also the values brought to bear both on the creation of sources and on their

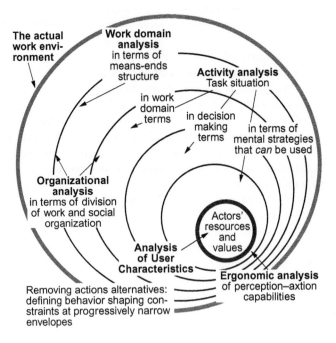

Figure 5.1 "Onion model" of cognitive work analysis (Rasmussen et al., 1994).

use. The next layer is an ergonomic analysis, which is to say literally an analysis of the work place (or, metaphorically, analysis of the work space) and of how the ergonomics affect or reflect perceptions nested in the actions of the participants. The next several layers involve analysis of specific actions, including tasks, decisions, and strategies. This is nested inside an analysis of the organization and how it embraces not only its actors and tasks, but also their values and perceptions and how those accord with or differ from organizational goals, values, and perceptions. The penultimate layer is the means-ends work domain analysis, in which all of the data gathered to this point are arrayed in terms of how they represent individual means and their contributions to individual ends. Of course, the large picture is not excluded and the collective means and ends also are analyzed. All of it is used to interpret the domain as a work environment. A concise report by Albrechtsen and Pejtersen (2003) was among the first to explain the use of the technique for generating work-based classifications.

Mai (2008) has produced the most cogent explanation of the CWA model and how it can be used in knowledge organization domain analysis for the generation of controlled vocabularies. Readers contemplating the use of CWA are strongly urged to consult his text directly and in detail. He extends the model by setting it inside the nested interpretation of information behavior, which is itself a symbolic shell surrounding information search behavior. In other words, it is neither sufficient merely to generate a domain's ontology, nor it is sufficient to analyze how its users make use of the ontology for specific information retrieval behavior. Rather, it is critical to understand the overall information behavior of the actors in terms of their information interactions, the constraints imposed by the domain, and the actors' attempts to deal with those constraints. In other words, symbolic interpretation of knowledge contexts is critical to explain the perceptual component of any domain ontology. And that understanding is crucial for the design and implementation of useful knowledge organization systems.

5.3 Two studies using CWA for knowledge organization

Albrechtsen et al. (2002) reported a study of collaborative film indexing. The actors working in a national film archives were analyzed not only in terms of searching and indexing tasks, but in the larger context of the work environment. In other words, the actors' collective (or collaborative) interpretations were seen as emergent from the specifically observed actions and narrative analysis of their decisions and decision-making processes. The ongoing nature of the actors' activities imports a richer perception of knowledge generation and use inside and outside the environment. Referring to the larger study, Albrechtsen and Pejtersen (2003, p. 223, emphasis original) conclude that "the strength of empirical analysis is the capture and formulation of structures *evolving amongst the collaborating actors*, irrespective of their knowledge levels and ability for articulating what they know, and just as importantly, do not know." As they also point out, the difficulty of generating work-based

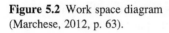

Figure 5.2 Work space diagram (Marchese, 2012, p. 63).

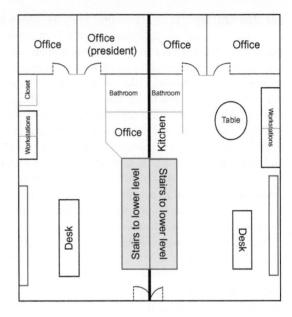

knowledge organization systems arises not from the task of eliciting the conceptual structure of the domain knowledge base, but rather from the fact that the shared semantics of that knowledge base constantly are shifting, evolving over time as the work shapes and reshapes the actors' perceptions.

A more recent study by Marchese (2012) employed the basic methodology of CWA to discover and trace the evolution of the knowledge base of a New York human relations firm. Marchese's report is a good source of clarity for her precise explanation of the implementation of the methodology. For example, the ergonomic analysis of the work domain was dependent on understanding the impact of the actual arrangement of work space in the firm. Figure 5.2 is a reproduction of the working floor plan observed by the researcher while inside the domain.

5.4 Qualitative analysis for greater perspective

What emerges from this brief introduction to qualitative approaches to domain analysis is the great richness that can be provided by the contextual perspective uncovered through qualitative methods. In Chapter 2, we mentioned the work by Hartel (2003, 2010) and Chaudhry and Ling (2005). Although these studies did not specifically incorporate the CWA methodology, all of them used work-based ethnographic analytical techniques to enrich understanding of the conceptual structure of specific domains. For every empirical study that elicits term lists and conceptual structures from the documentary evidence of a domain, researchers should see an opportunity to expand contextual understanding by working inside the domain, alongside its actors.

References

Albrechtsen, H., Pejtersen, A.M., 2003. Cognitive work analysis and work centered design of classification schemes. Knowl. Organ. 30, 213–227.

Albrechtsen, H., Pejtersen, A.M., Cleal, B., 2002. Empirical work analysis of collaborative film indexing. In: Bruce, H., Fidel, R., Ingwersen, P., Vakkari, P. (Eds.), Emerging Frameworks and Methods: Proceedings of the Fourth International Conference on Conceptions of Library and Information Science. Libraries Unlimited, Greenwood Village, CO, pp. 85–108.

Blumer, H., 1969. Symbolic Interactionism: Perspective and Method. University of California Press, Berkeley.

Chaudhry, A.S., Ling, G.H., 2005. Building taxonomies using organizational resources: a case of business consulting environment. Knowl. Organ. 32, 25–46.

Hartel, J., 2003. The serious leisure frontier in library and information science: hobby domains. Knowl. Organ. 30, 228–238.

Hartel, J., 2010. Managing documents at home for serious leisure: a case study of the hobby of gourmet cooking. J. Doc. 66, 847–874.

Mai, J.-E., 2008. Design and construction of controlled vocabularies: analysis of actors, domain, and constraints. Knowl. Organ. 35, 16–29.

Marchese, C., 2012. Impact of organizational environment on knowledge representation and use: cognitive work analysis of a management consulting firm. Ph.D. dissertation. Long Island University.

Rasmussen, J., Pejtersen, A.M., Goodstein, L.P., 1994. Cognitive Systems Engineering. Wiley, New York, NY.

Vicente, K., 1999. Cognitive Work Analysis: Toward Safe, Productive, and Healthy Computer-based Work. Lawrence Erlbaum, Hillsdale.

Conclusions

6.1 Domain analysis has evolved in the KO community

We have seen how domain analysis arose from roots in information science to become a core methodological paradigm in the science of knowledge organization. The purpose of knowledge organization is to discover and order knowledge bases in the form of transferable ontologies. The use of domain analysis is the primary approach to concept discovery, semantic interpretation, and the comprehension of contextual priorities for knowledge ordering in functioning communities. We have analyzed the rapid growth of the use of domain analysis in the formal publication venues of knowledge organization and isolated a core evolutionary literature. We have examined in some detail sources for domain analysis, in particular for the analysis of trace evidence provided by references in the formal papers of scholarly domains. A set of core empirical techniques for eliciting term sets at different taxonomic levels as well as for comprehending their symbolic or perceptual contexts was explored. These are primarily citation analysis, coword analysis, author cocitation analysis, and network analysis, and on the qualitative side, cognitive work analysis. Historical, epistemological, and genre analyses, and analyses using critical theory, including discourse analyses, were not discussed in detail because they do not rely on straightforward, observable, and replicable techniques for term extraction and ontology orientation. These approaches rely on the analysis of a wide variety of artifacts, including documents, for secondary evidence that can be used to understand the intellectual functioning of domains and are better comprehended from their originating domains of history, philosophy, and sociology.

In the course of analyzing the formal research of domain analysis for knowledge organization, we were able to generate a revised taxonomy of approaches. These are:

- Subject pathfinders
- Special classifications and thesauri
- Empirical user studies
- Informetric studies
- Historical studies
- Document and genre studies
- Epistemological and critical studies
- Terminological studies
- Database semantics
- Discourse analyses
- Cognition, expert knowledge, and AI

It is clear that the knowledge organization community has embraced domain analysis as a scholarly methodological paradigm for the discovery of ontological bases and for the continuing analysis of the evolution of scholarly communities. The introduction of qualitative methods and particularly of discourse analysis have helped to enrich the contextual understanding of the functions, activities, shared semantics, and evolving constraints of knowledge-based domains. There has been little applied research, however, reporting the development or evolution of pathfinders or subject gateways, even in the face of expanding digital hegemony over all human activity. This volume contains a thorough analysis of the first decade of the formal use of domain analysis in the knowledge organization community. The analysis here also points directly toward the need for a future expansion of domain-analytical research.

6.2   What we have learned from KO domain analysis

At the end of Chapter 2, we visited some summary data about the extent of domain analysis reported in the formal venues of the field of knowledge organization. Nearly 100 research reports were analyzed, and these reported on investigations of more than 50 different domains. While more than 30 domains were studied only once in this corpus, these domains were studied more than once:

- Studied twice: astronomy, cooking, Chinese information science, digital libraries, the Dublin Core Metadata Initiative, the *Encyclopedia of Milwaukee*, gender studies, nursing, race, and tripsanomatides.
- Studied three times: archives, image searching, LGBT communities, physics, and social media.

Music was studied four times. There were 22 studies of aspects of knowledge organization. The result is obvious: we have studied our own domain in detail, but we have studied few other domains adequately for either knowledge discovery or development of knowledge organization systems. Figure 6.1 is developed by cross tabulating the years of study and the numbers of studies with the eleven formal approaches to domain analysis across three formal venues (ISKO Proceedings in the series *Advances in Knowledge Organization* (*AIKO*), *Knowledge Organization* the journal, and other information science journals (ISJ in the figure)).

A quick glimpse at the figure shows that most domain-analytical studies have relied on metric techniques, mostly forms of citation analysis. Quite a few empirical user studies also are reported, as are discourse analyses. Few historical analyses or documentary studies have appeared. Progress has been steady in all the three venues, and the number of studies has increased over time in all venues. Most of the studies in information science journals are in some way metric. Special classifications and thesauri are more often reported in *Knowledge Organization*. Discourse analysis is more common in conference proceedings, suggesting more such studies should be extended for reporting in formal journal venues.

There is also little sense to the mix of domains that have been studied, and the majority have been studied only once. Where three or four studies in a domain have occurred, it would be useful for new studies to begin with meta-analyses of the prior studies so as to generate cumulative knowledge and understanding of these domains. Few of the formal sciences have been studied—astronomy and physics are notable. But it remains likely that most such studies are reported in domain-centric venues

Number of approaches by year by venue: Count

		Approach									
Venue	Year	Cognition, AI	Document and genre study	Empirical user study	Epistemo logical and critical	Historical study	Informetric study	Literature guide or subject..	Special classification or th..	Terminology or discourse..	Terminology or discourse..
AIKO	2004	1		1	1			1			1
	2006			1	1		1			1	1
	2008			1			1			1	
	2010	1	1	1	3		1			1	2
	2012			1			6			1	
	2014			1			4	1		3	
ISJ	1995						1				
	2005						1				
	2007								1		
	2008						2				
	2010										1
	2011			1	1		1	1			1
	2012						1				
	2013			1			1	1	1		1
KO	2004			3	2					1	
	2005								1		
	2007			2	1						
	2008								1	1	
	2009					1			1		
	2010								1		
	2011				1						
	2012		2				1				
	2013			1		3			2		
	2014			3		1	4		2		

Sum of count broken down by approach vs. venue and year.

Figure 6.1 A decade of domain analysis in KO.

and not, therefore, as analyses amenable to use for knowledge organization without further analysis. Much replication is needed, but also the knowledge organization community needs to engage in more detailed search for domain-analytical results in the formal venues of other domains.

6.3 Using existing evidence to generate domain analysis

In Chapter 1, I made reference to Impressionist artists, based on a quotation by Gladwell (2013) from a work by White and White (1992). As it happens, the work by White and White could easily be viewed as a prelude to domain analysis of the French painting world. In the opening of the book, the authors define an institutional system in terms quite reminiscent of my own definition of a domain (pp. 2–4):

> A persistent network of beliefs, customs, and formal procedures which together form a
> more-or-less articulated social organization with an acknowledged central purpose—
> here the creation and recognition of art. The purpose is realized through recruitment,
> training, continuous indoctrination, a sequential process of appraisal and graded
> recognition, regularized appropriation of economic support from the environment,
> a graded system of discipline and punishment, acknowledge machinery for

*legitimation of adaptation and change, and controlled communication with the social
environment. Each of these functions implies some set of subsidiary roles marginal
between the institutional system and its social environment, as well as some role
structure in the world of painters themselves.*

In other words, the domain of the institutional system of French painting involved a
community with a common teleology, shared epistemology, shared work, and shared
products. The community concretized around methods of control and legitimation that
served as points of entry (or discharge) for acceptable work. The afterword to the 1993
edition of the book lays out in some detail how the evolution of the domain led to
cumulative canonical change. Much of the data in Chapter 4 of the book, which is
about the role of the Impressionist painters in this evolution, presents quantitative data
about the means by which these painters worked not as revolutionaries, but as agents
of change from inside their domain.

My point is that scholarship of all kinds is replete with quantification of domains
and the evolution of their knowledge bases. The knowledge organization community
would do well to begin to seek to extrapolate domain data from the communities in
which it is being generated, so as to apply these data to the evolution of knowledge
organization systems. Dahlberg (2009, 2011) has suggested much the same. Among
her stated desiderata for the field of knowledge organization are the realization that the
concept and the word, the knowledge unit and the term, are fundamentally different. It
is here that the contextual value of multitheory and multimethods approaches to
domain analysis can broaden the terminological base of many existing systems for
knowledge organization. Also among her desiderata is a call for detailed systematic
analysis of extant knowledge organization systems in all domains in order to discover
and incorporate relevant conceptual elements.

Specifically, in 2009 she laid out fundamental steps that knowledge organization
must now undertake the field through its embrace of domain analysis. Here are three
figures from that paper, in which we find all of the steps of domain analysis
(Figure 6.2).

First we must conceive of domains as epistemological moments in the universe of
items. In this she agrees with Hjørland that all knowledge organization artifacts are the
result of the activity of domains. She suggests that we must distinguish between the
universe of items as an abstraction, and the reality of the predicates of entities (items in
her terms) of conceptual importance to a domain (Figure 6.3).

Here we see Dahlberg inviting us to investigate not just conceptual entities, but also
their contexts, their properties, the activities from which they are derived, and the
dimensions in which they are extant. These are epistemological questions (Figure 6.4).

Here is Dahlberg's functional list of questions for the empirical side of domain
analysis; both quantitative and qualitative designs are implied in this series of questions. We are charged to investigate not only that which we can observe easily and

```
Universe of items
Objects, activities, properties, themes, etc.


A                          Item of reference



B      Whole of predicates on the item of reference,
              determination of its characteristics


C                  Summarizing designation
            for the statements, the characteristics


              Utilization of the designation
              in the universe of discourse
```

Figure 6.2 Dahlberg's conceptualization of a chosen domain (Dahlberg, 2009, p. 171).

```
                     Abstract entities
(1) Entities         Concrete entities
                     Principles


                     Quantity
(2) Properties       Quality
                     Relation (in the sense of comparison)


                     Operation (active)
(3) Activities       Process (procedure)
                     State (passive, zero-activity)


                     Time
(4) Dimensions       Space
                     Position
```

Figure 6.3 Dahlberg's categories in Aristotelian terms (Dahlberg, 2009, p. 172).

empirically, but then also to challenge our assumptions by asking "What if?," "Why?," "For what purpose?," and 14 other questions. Dahlberg here is directing the science of knowledge organization to move more deeply into the metadisciplinary space of what she has seen as a science of science. Therein lies the future of the science of knowledge organization.

Questions	Categories	Latin questions
1. What if?	Possibility	utrum?
2. What?	Nature, essence	quid?
3. From what?	Material stuff, substance	de quo?
4. Why?	Causality, reason	quare?
5. How big?	Quantity, size	quantum?
6. How good?	Quality	quale?
7. When? Since when?	Time	quando?
8. Where? From where?	Place	ubi?
9. How? In which way?	Modality	quomodo?
10. By which means?	Instrumentality	cum quo?
11. By what?	Potentiality, capability	
12. How generated?	Genesis	
13. By whom?	Originator, producer	
14. With whom?	Accompanied by, together with	
15. For what purpose?	Finality	
16. How occurring?	Occurrence, in parallel, in connection	
17. Under which condition?	Condition	

Figure 6.4 Dahlberg's functional domain-analytical questions (Dahlberg, 2009, p. 173).

References

Dahlberg, I., 2009. Concepts and terms: ISKO's major challenge. Knowl. Organ. 36, 169–177.

Dahlberg, I., 2011. How to improve ISKO's standing: ten desiderata for knowledge organization. Knowl. Organ. 38, 68–74.

Gladwell, M., 2013. David and Goliath: Underdogs, Misfits, and the Art of Battling Giants. Little, Brown, New York.

White, H., White, C., 1992. Canvases and Careers; Institutional Change in the French Painting World, with a New Foreword and a New Afterword. University of Chicago Press ed. In: University of Chicago Press, Chicago.

Index

Note: Page numbers followed by *f* indicate figures and *t* indicate tables.

Printed and bound by CPI Group (UK) Ltd, Croydon, CR0 4YY

08/06/2025

01896869-0007